Piano / Vocal / Guitar

JASON MRAZ **YES!**

ISBN 978-1-4803-9508-4

HAL•LEONARD®
CORPORATION

7777 W. BLUEMOUND RD. P.O. BOX 13819 MILWAUKEE, WI 53213

In Australia Contact:
Hal Leonard Australia Pty. Ltd.
4 Lentara Court
Cheltenham, Victoria, 3192 Australia
Email: ausadmin@halleonard.com.au

Visit Hal Leonard Online at
www.halleonard.com

RISE

Words and Music by JASON MRAZ, BECKY GEBHARDT,
CHASKA POTTER, MAI BLOOMFIELD, MONA TAVAKOLI,
CHRIS KEUP and STEWART MYERS

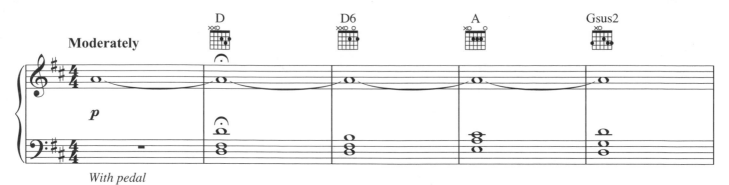

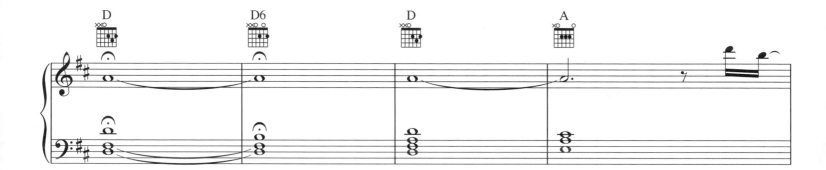

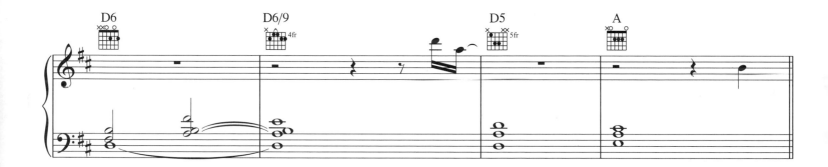

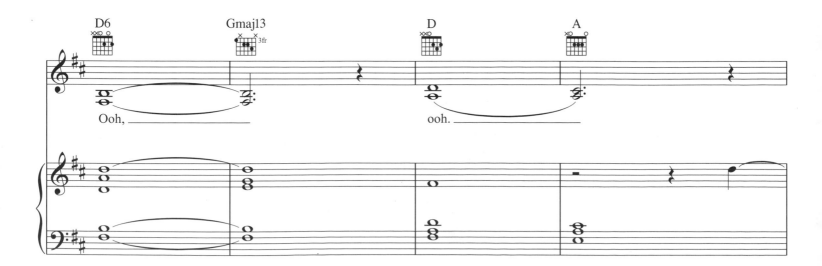

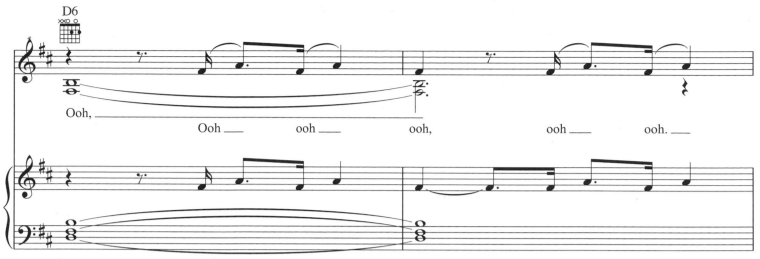

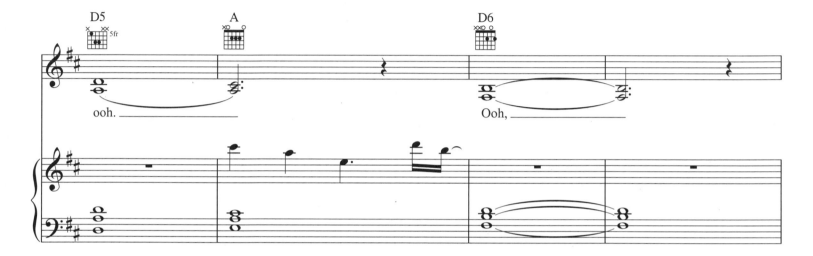

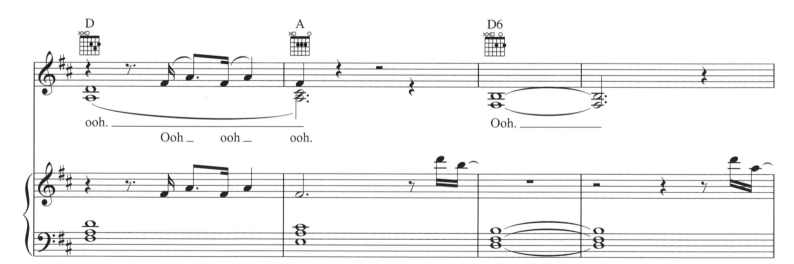

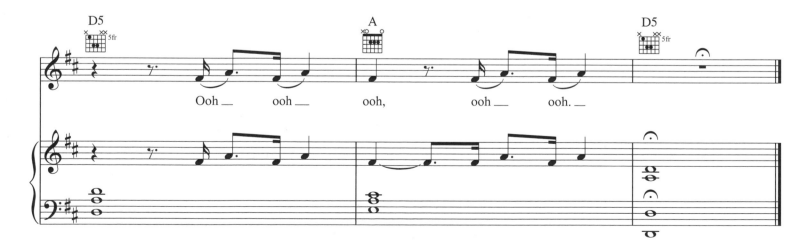

LOVE SOMEONE

Words and Music by JASON MRAZ,
BECKY GEBHARDT, CHASKA POTTER,
MAI BLOOMFIELD, MONA TAVAKOLI,
CHRIS KEUP and STEWART MYERS

whole heart as my heart re - ceives your

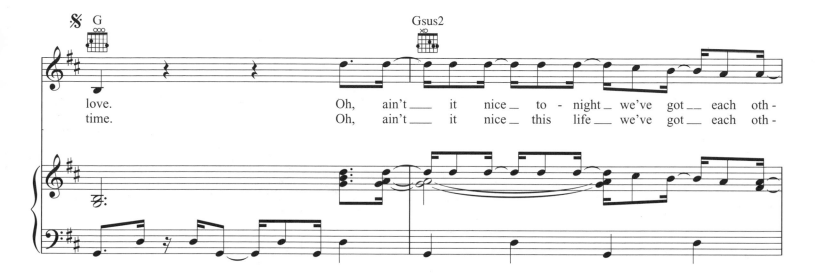

love.
time.

Oh, ain't ___ it nice ___ to - night ___ we've got ___ each oth -
Oh, ain't ___ it nice ___ this life ___ we've got ___ each oth -

- er? ___
- er? ___

And I am

right be - side you, more than just ___ a part - ner or a lov -

-er; ____ I'm __ your friend. When you _ love ____ some -

one, ____ your heart-beat beats so loud. ____ When you __ love __

____ some - one, ____ your feet can't feel the ground. _

Ooh, shin - y __ stars ____ all seem to

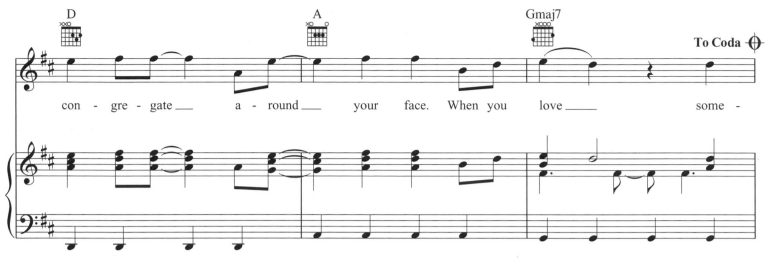

To Coda

con - gre - gate a - round your face. When you love some -

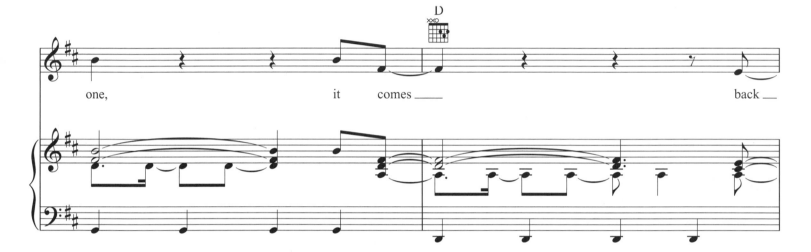

one, it comes back

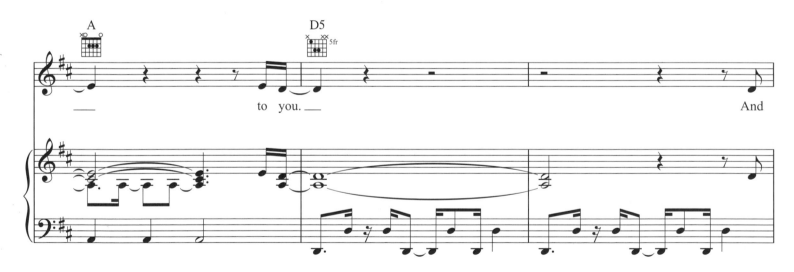

to you. And

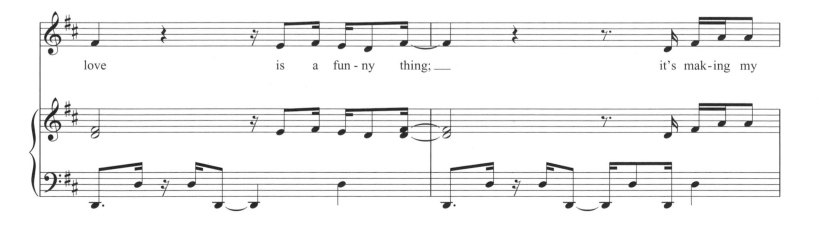

love is a fun - ny thing; it's mak-ing my

blood flow with en - er - gy. _____ And this

life, an a - wak - ing _____ dream, is what I've been

D.S. al Coda

wish - ing for is hap - pen - ing. _____ And it's right on

CODA

A

one, when _ you love some - one...

We're gon - na give___ our - selves___ to love___ to - night,___

lift - ing up___ to touch___ the star - light. Now, we will

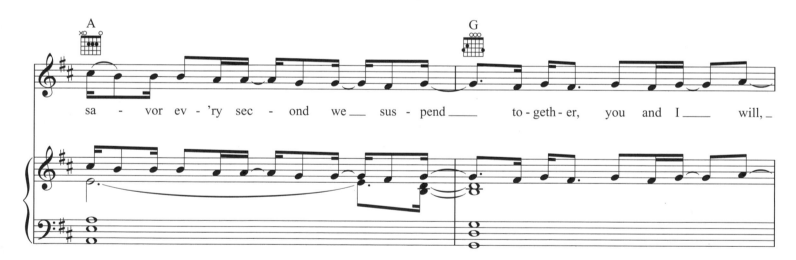

sa - vor ev - 'ry sec - ond we___ sus - pend___ to - geth - er, you and I___ will,___

___ you and I___ will,___ you and I___ will.___

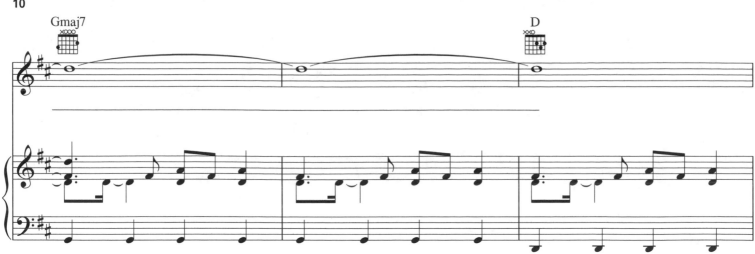

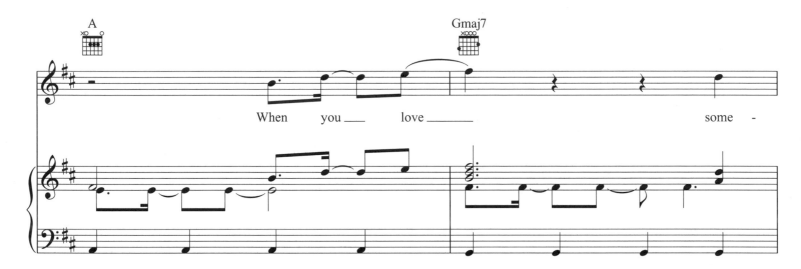

When you ___ love _____ some -

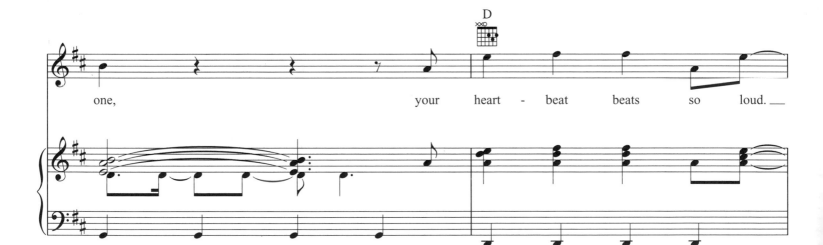

one, your heart - beat beats so loud. ___

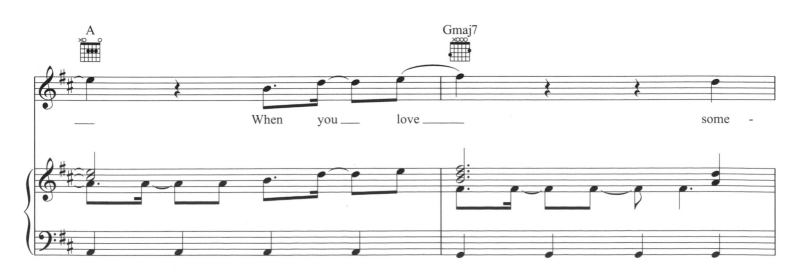

When you ___ love _____ some -

one, your feet can't feel the ground. ___

Ooh, shin-y ___ stars ___ all seem to con-gre-gate ___ a-round ___

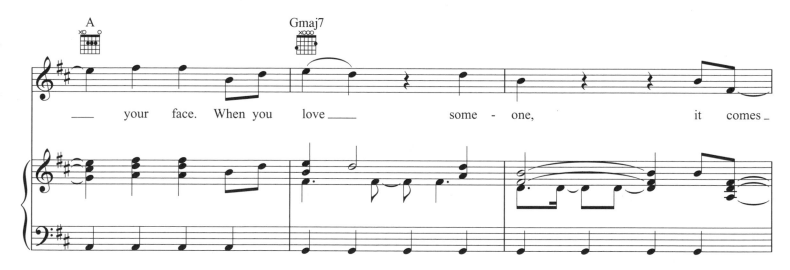

___ your face. When you love ___ some-one, it comes ___

___ back ___ to you. ___

HELLO YOU BEAUTIFUL THING

`Words and Music by JASON MRAZ,
BECKY GEBHARDT, CHASKA POTTER
and MONA TAVAKOLI

Fall out of bed and catch a

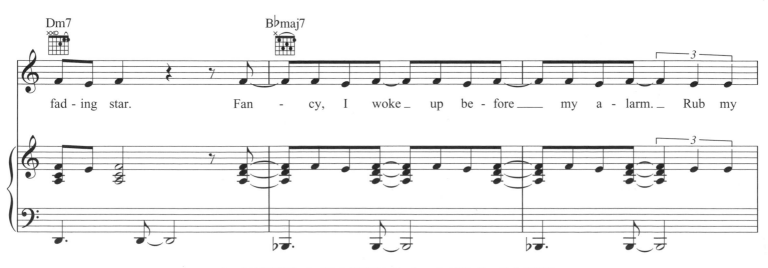

fad - ing star.   Fan - cy, I woke_ up be - fore___ my a - larm.___ Rub my

mind through my eyes, ___ it's the best ___ I can do be - fore it's

au - to - mat - ic hab - it of re - tur - ning to you, ___ though I smile ___

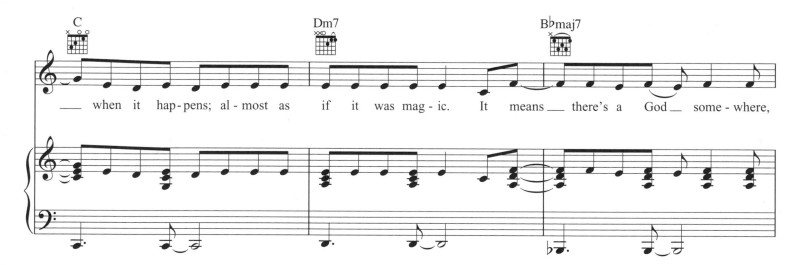

___ when it hap - pens; al - most as if it was mag - ic. It means ___ there's a God ___ some - where,

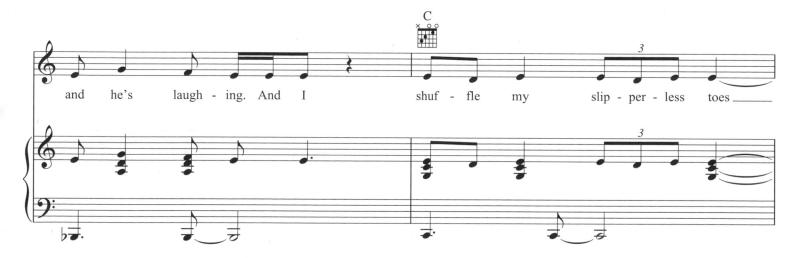

and he's laugh - ing. And I shuf - fle my slip - per - less toes ___

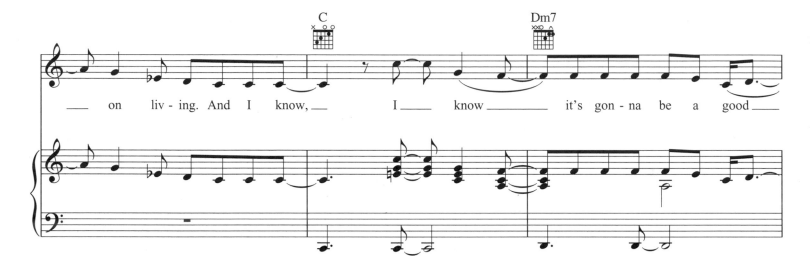

lo, hel - lo, _____ you beau - ti - ful _____ thing.

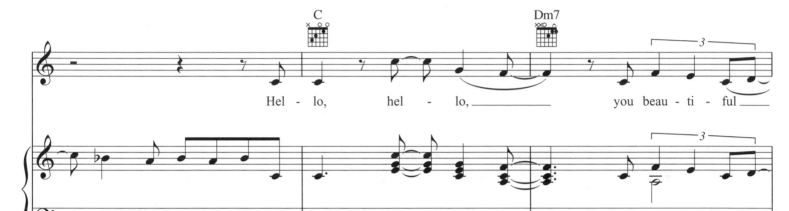

Hel - lo, hel - lo, _____ you beau - ti - ful _____

_____ thing. {Oh, This} is what I've been
              {   this}

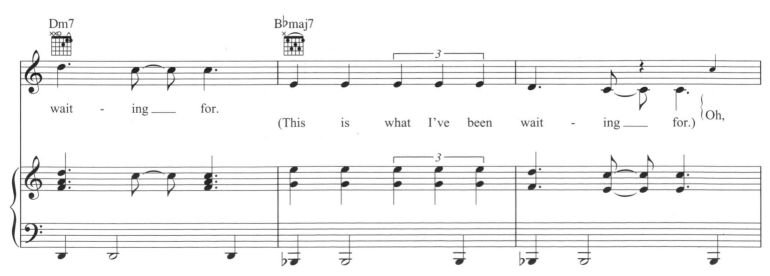

wait - ing _____ for.

(This is what I've been wait - ing _____ for.) {Oh,

This (This is) is what I've been wait - ing for. (This is what I've been

wait - ing for.)

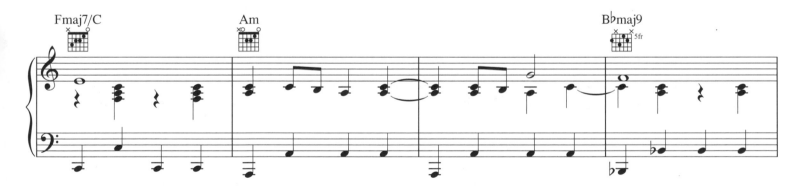

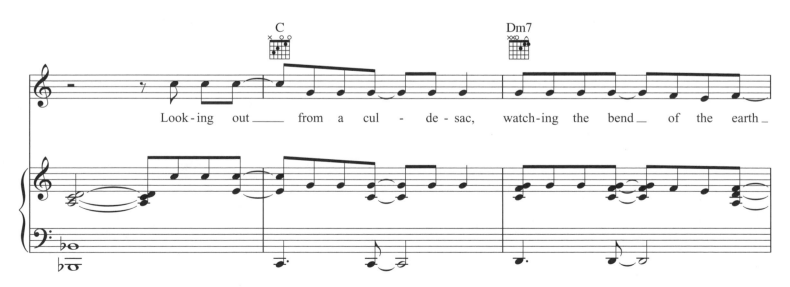

Look - ing out from a cul - de - sac, watch-ing the bend of the earth

B♭maj7

take the black of the night from the dirt. I can see

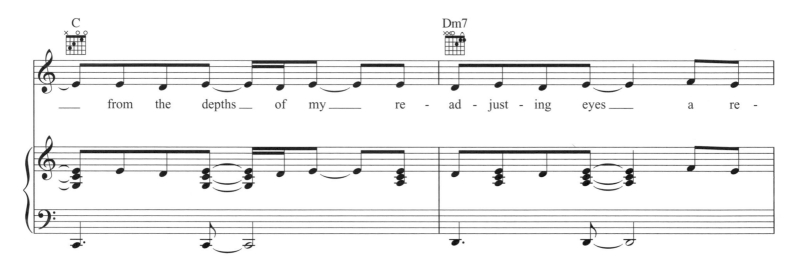

C Dm7

from the depths of my re - ad - just - ing eyes a re -

B♭maj7 C

flec - tion of yes - ses in that ev - er-chang-ing sky. But why do bad dreams lin-ger long af -

Dm7 B♭maj7

ter I a - wake? I don't need no scenes of vio - lence or pain

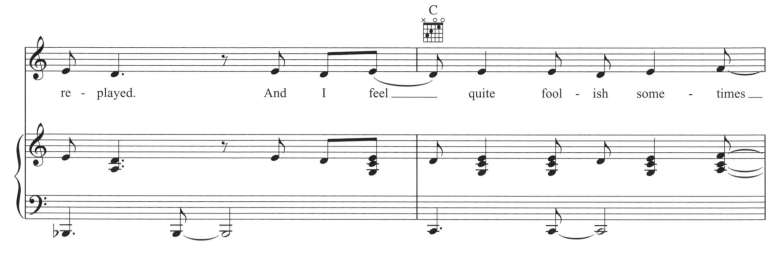

re - played. And I feel _____ quite fool - ish some - times _____

_____ when I pray, but my thoughts _____ are all I've got, so I try

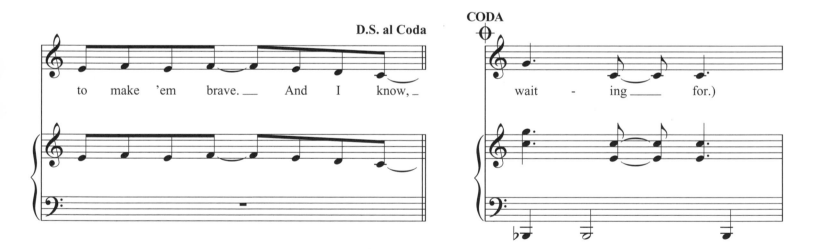

to make 'em brave. _____ And I know, _____ wait - ing _____ for.)

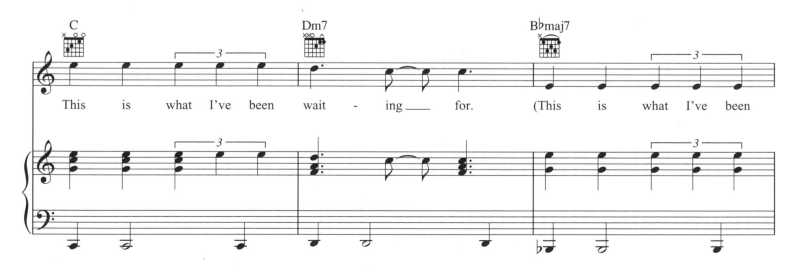

This is what I've been wait - ing _____ for. (This is what I've been

LONG DRIVE

Words and Music by JASON MRAZ,
BECKY GEBHARDT, CHASKA POTTER,
MAI BLOOMFIELD and MONA TAVAKOLI

Moderately slow half-time feel

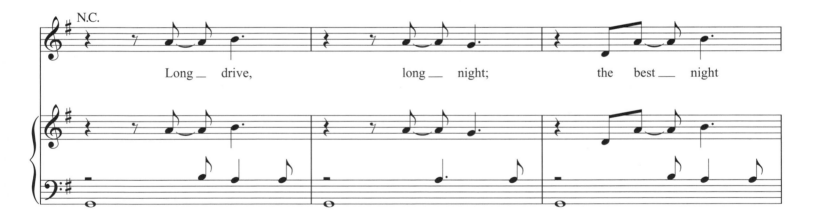

Long ___ drive,   long ___ night;   the best ___ night

of my ___ life.   With ___ you   rid - ing,

your __ hand on my __ hand. The thought of

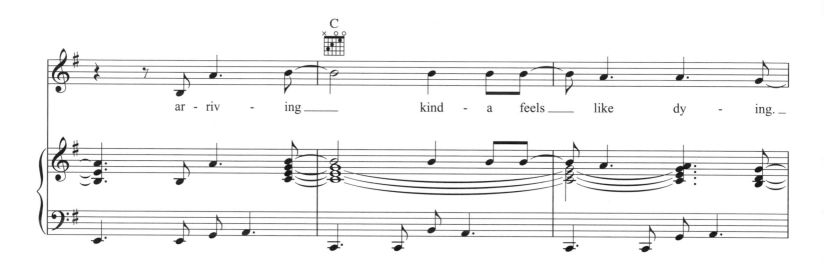

ar - riv - ing ____ kind - a feels ____ like dy - ing. __

__ I don't want ____ to go home ____ and be

a - lone. Could __ we stay __ out?

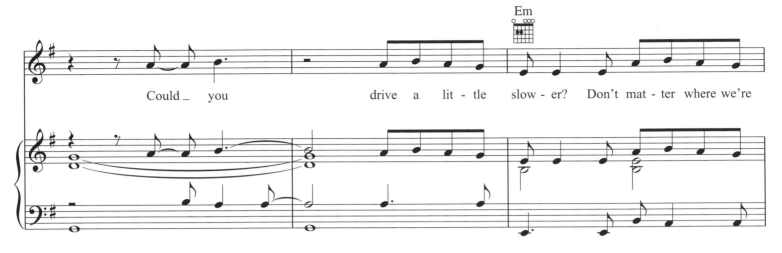

Could you drive a lit-tle slow-er? Don't mat-ter where we're

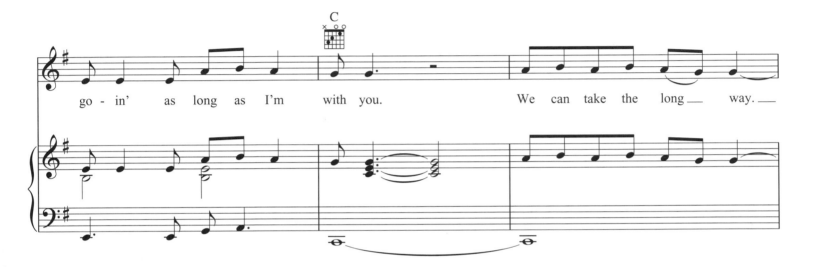

go-in' as long as I'm with you. We can take the long way.

Chev-y No-va; front seat

so - fa.   Get - ting   clos - er

to ___ you.   Drive a lit - tle slow - er; don't mat - ter where we're

go - in' as long as I'm with you.   We can take the long __ way. __

_____   Drive a lit - tle

slow - er; not read - y to go home, I'd rath - er stay with you. ____

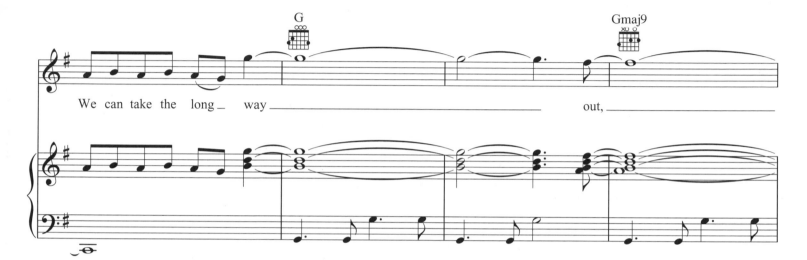

We can take the long ___ way ____ out, ____

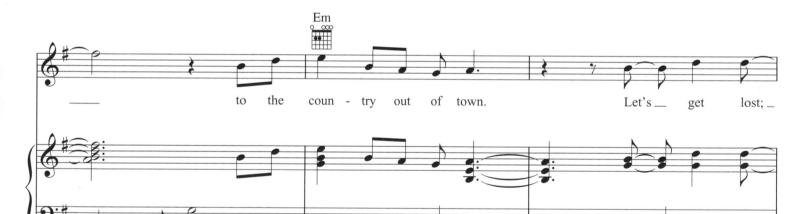

____ to the coun - try out of town. Let's ___ get lost; ___

____ I don't wan - na be found. ___ Let's ___ get a - way, ____

now. And be care - ful not to crash;

there's no de - frost, and we're steam- in' the glass. You and the road

have a gen- er -ous shoul - der. We could pull o - ver, and

Driving 4 feel

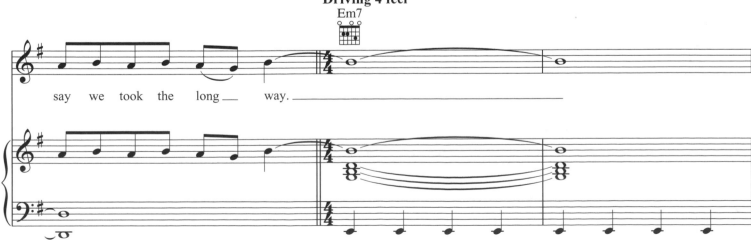

say we took the long way.

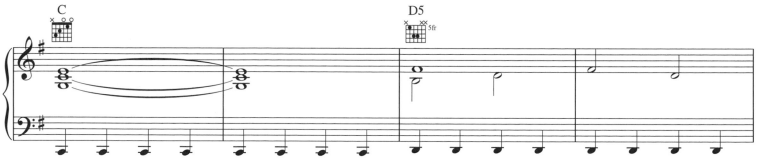

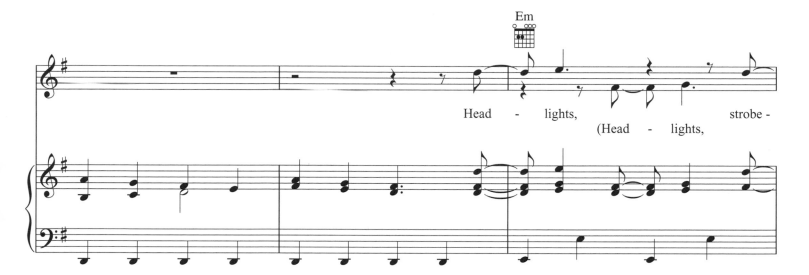

Head - lights, strobe -
(Head - lights,

- lights. I see ___ you, well, not ___ quite. I can feel ___
strobe - lights. See ___ you, not ___ quite.

___ you in - side. Time ___ is ___ Time ___ is just ___
Feel ___ you in - side.

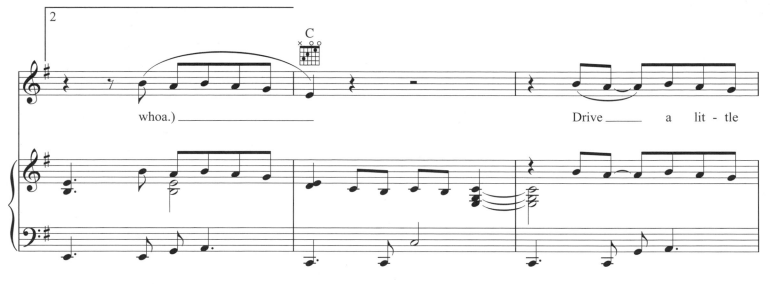

whoa.) _____ Drive _____ a lit - tle

slow - er; don't mat - ter where we're go - in', go - in', now. _____ (Whoa.) _

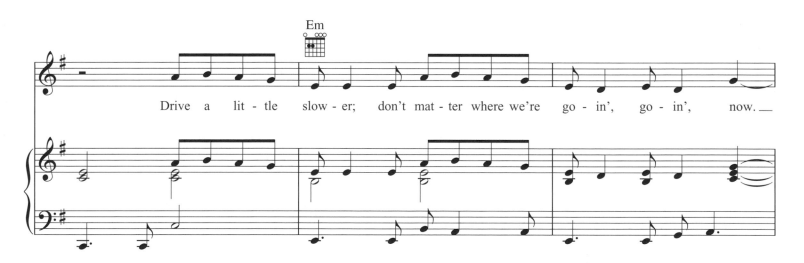

Drive a lit - tle slow - er; don't mat - ter where we're go - in', go - in', now. _

_ (Whoa.) _____ Drive a lit - tle slow - er; not read - y to go

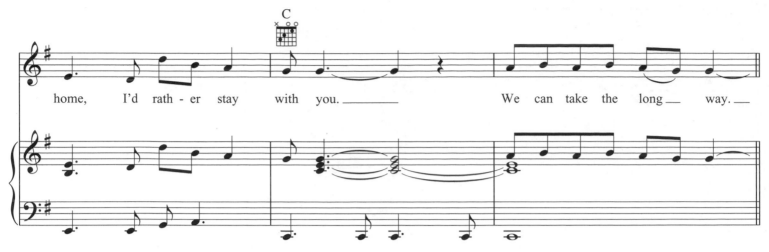

home, I'd rath - er stay with you. _____ We can take the long ___ way. ___

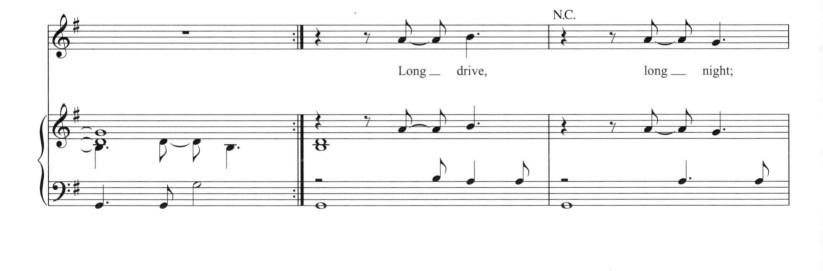

Long ___ drive, long ___ night;

the best ___ night of my ___ life. _____

EVERYWHERE

Words and Music by JASON MRAZ,
BECKY GEBHARDT, CHASKA POTTER,
MAI BLOOMFIELD and MONA TAVAKOLI

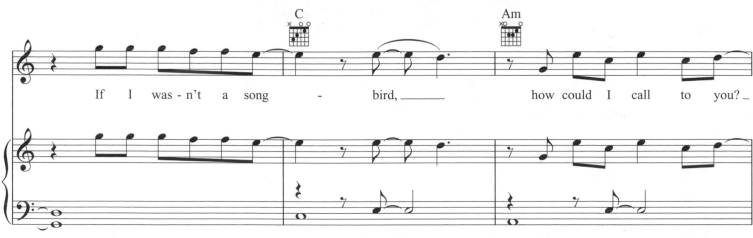

If I was-n't a song - bird, how could I call to you?

If I was-n't a fly on the wall, I would-n't

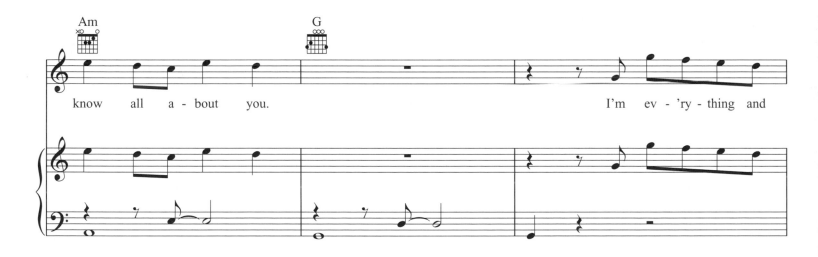

know all a - bout you. I'm ev - 'ry - thing and

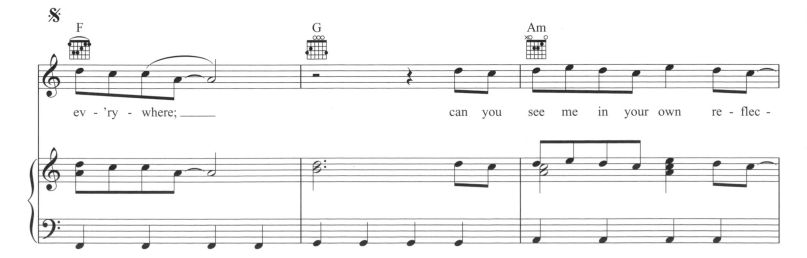

ev - 'ry - where; can you see me in your own re - flec -

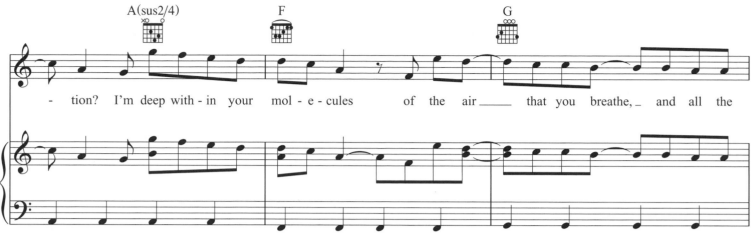

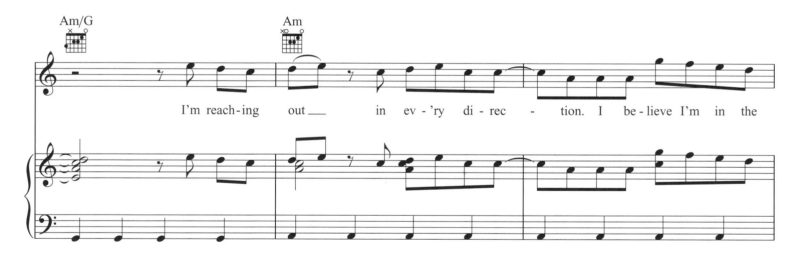

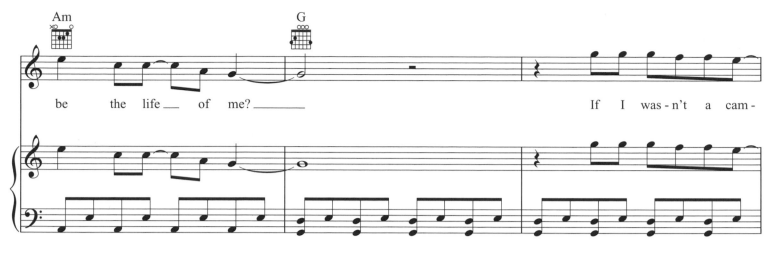

be the life __ of me? _____ If I was-n't a cam-

- er - a, ___ how could you be so pho-to-gen-ic? Yeah, I said it!

If I was-n't the hands ___ on a clock, __ how could you

D.S. al Coda

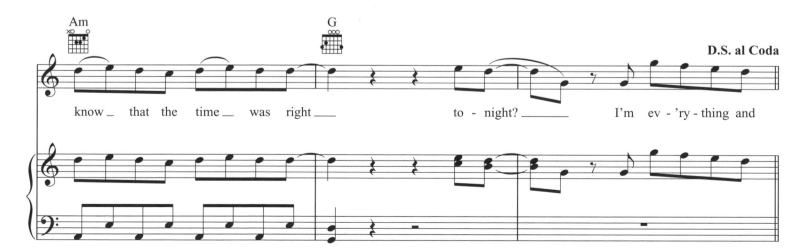

know __ that the time __ was right ___ to-night? _____ I'm ev-'ry-thing and

CODA

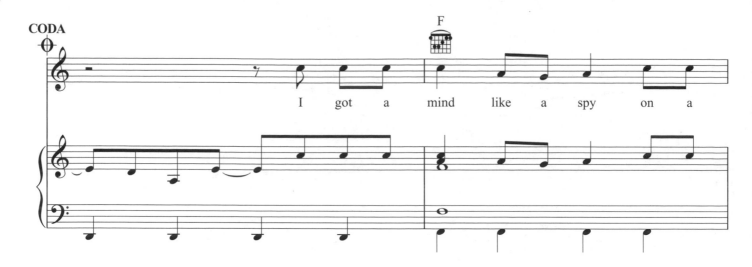

I got a mind like a spy on a

sat-el-lite check-ing you out. ___ I'm like a fly with my in-fi-nite eyes. ___ I can see

with all my sens-es and I'm com-ing to get you. I'm in-

vis-i-ble, ex-pand-a-ble and om-ni-pres-ent. I'm ev-

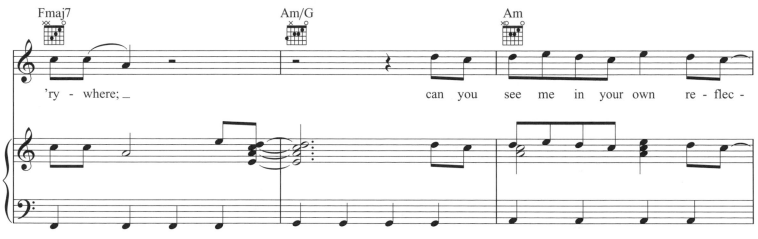

'ry - where; _ can you see me in your own re - flec -

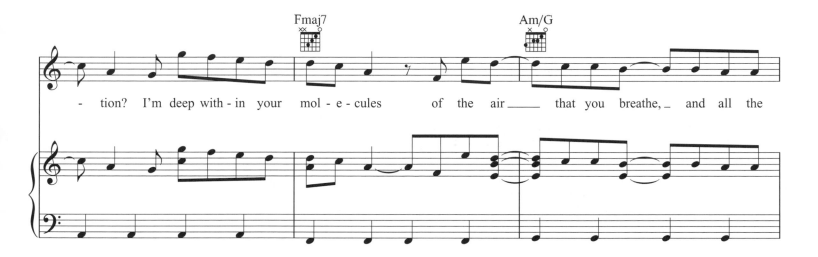

- tion? I'm deep with - in your mol - e - cules of the air ____ that you breathe, _ and all the

sub - a - tom - ic su - per - son - ic spac - es in be - tween. I'm ev -

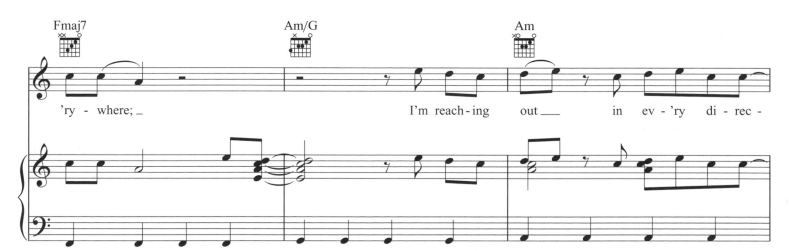

'ry - where; _ I'm reach - ing out ____ in ev - 'ry di - rec -

-tion. I be-lieve I'm in the wat-er, too, 'cause you act____ just like____ you need____

____ me. _____   I'm ev-'ry-where. _

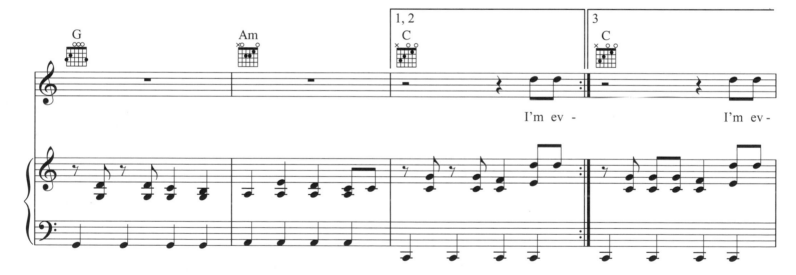

I'm ev-   I'm ev-

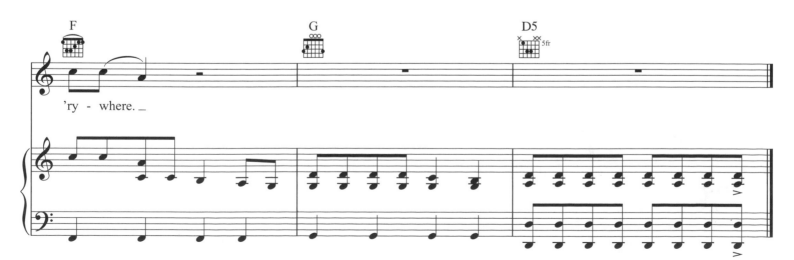

'ry - where. _

BEST FRIEND

Words and Music by JASON MRAZ,
BECKY GEBHARDT, CHASKA POTTER,
MAI BLOOMFIELD and MONA TAVAKOLI

Moderately slow groove

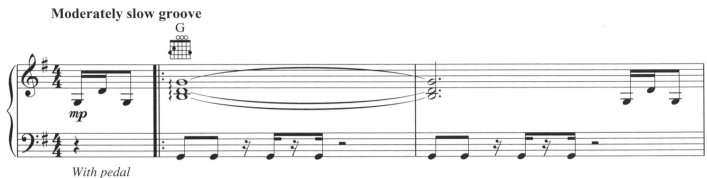

With pedal

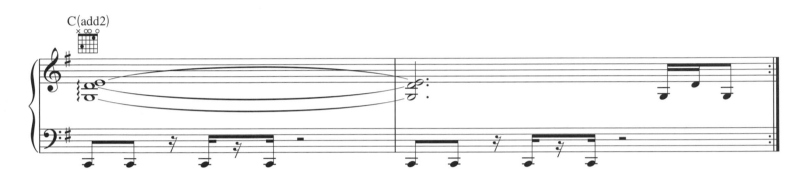

Love is where this be - gins; _____
Thank you for all of your trust. _____

thank you for let - ting me _____ in. _____
Thank you for not giv - ing _____ up. _____

I nev - er had to pre - tend; ____
Thank you for hold - ing my hand. ____

you've al - ways known who I ____ am. ____ And I know ____
I've al - ways known where you ____ stand. ____ Yes, I feel ____

____ my life ____ is bet - ter ____ be-cause you're ____ a part ____ of it. I know ____

____ with - out ____ you by ____ my side ____ that I ____ would be dif - fer - ent. ____

my life __ is bet - ter; __ so is the world __ we're liv - ing in. __ I'm

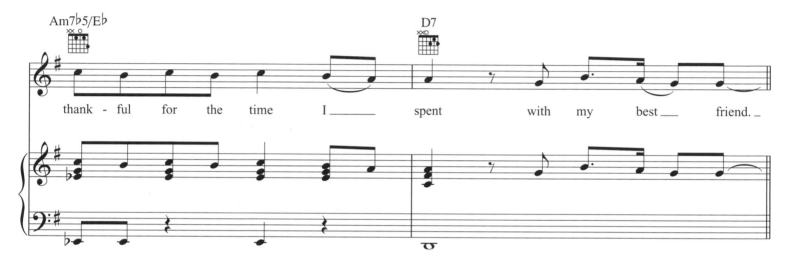

thank - ful for the time I _____ spent with my best __ friend. _

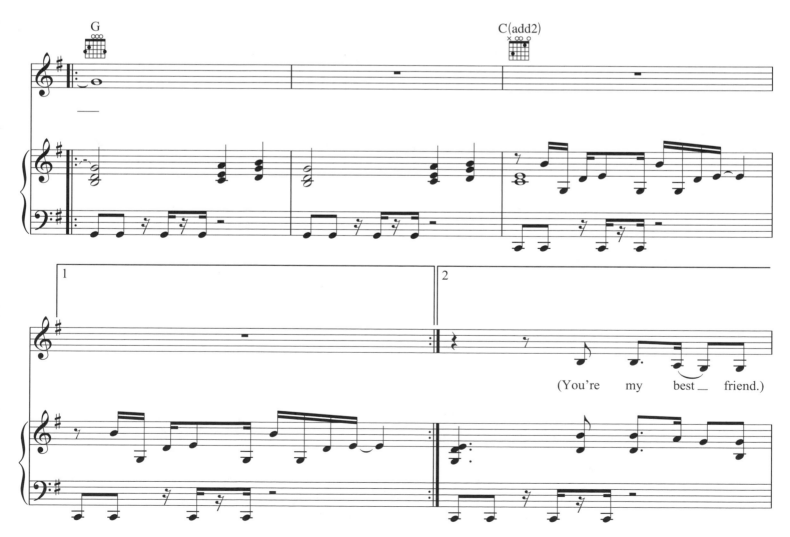

(You're my best __ friend.)

Thank you for call-ing me out. Thank you for wak-ing me up.

Thank you for break-ing it ___ down. Thank you for choos-ing us. ___

Thank you for all you're a-bout. Thank you for lift-ing me up.

Thank you for keep-ing me ground-ed, ___ and be-ing here ___ now. ___

My life is bet-ter be-cause you're a part of it. Yes, I know

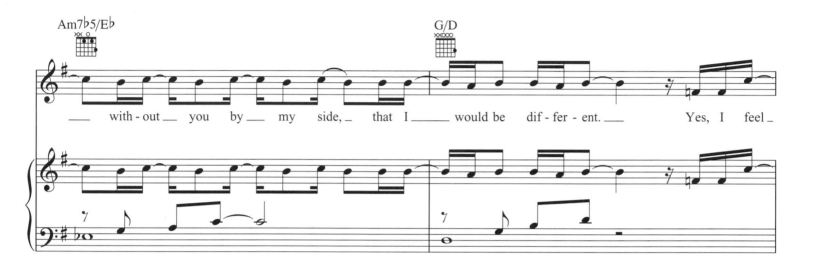

with-out you by my side, that I would be dif-fer-ent. Yes, I feel

my life is bet-ter, and so is the world we're liv-ing in. I'm

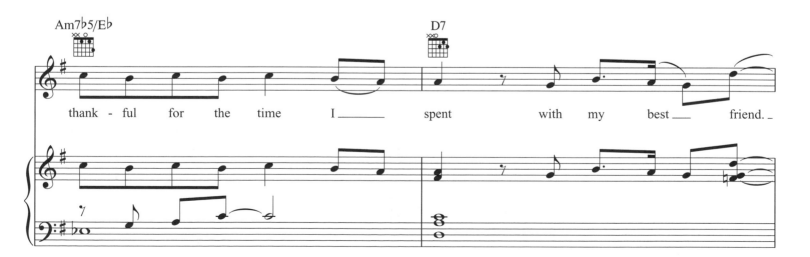

thank-ful for the time I spent with my best friend.

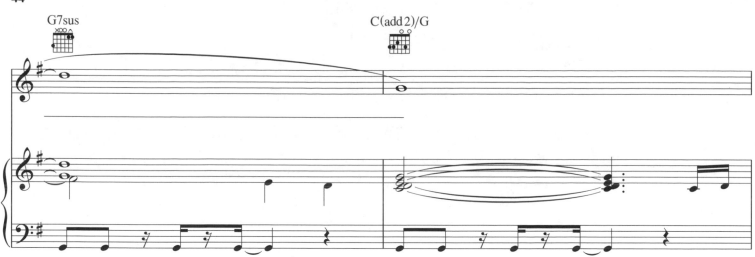

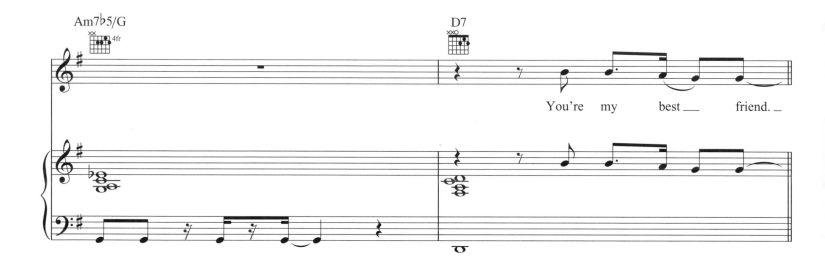

You're my best ___ friend. ___

QUIET

Words and Music by JASON MRAZ,
DANIEL OMELIO and AMMAR MALIK

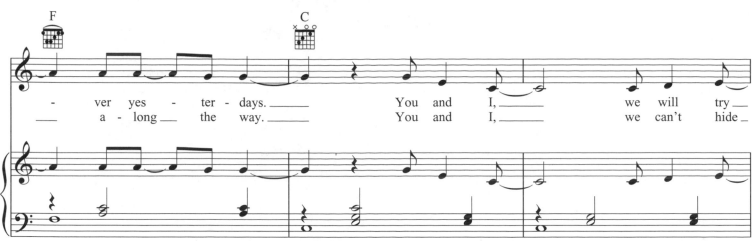

- ver yes - ter - days. _____ You and I, _____ we will try ___
- a - long ___ the way. _____ You and I, _____ we can't hide __

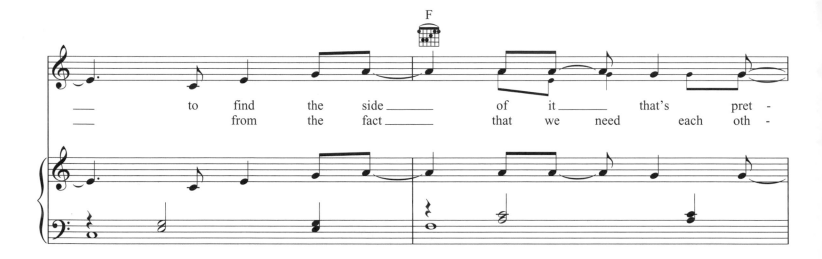

___ to find the side _____ of it _____ that's pret -
___ from the fact _____ that we need each oth -

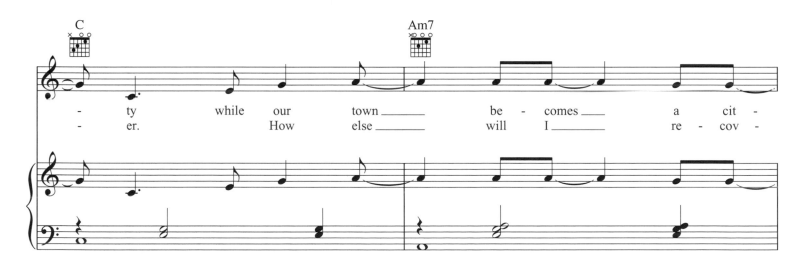

- ty while our town _____ be - comes ____ a cit -
- er. How else _____ will I _____ re - cov -

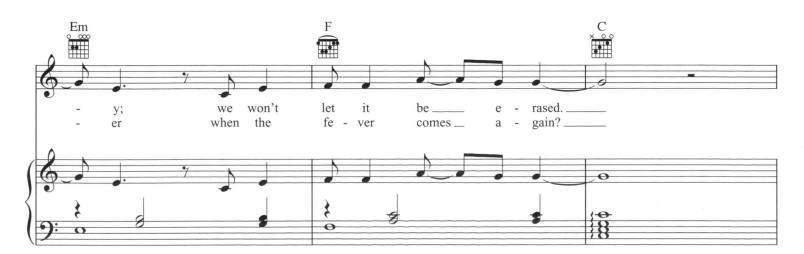

- y; we won't let it be ____ e - rased. _____
- er when the fe - ver comes __ a - gain? _____

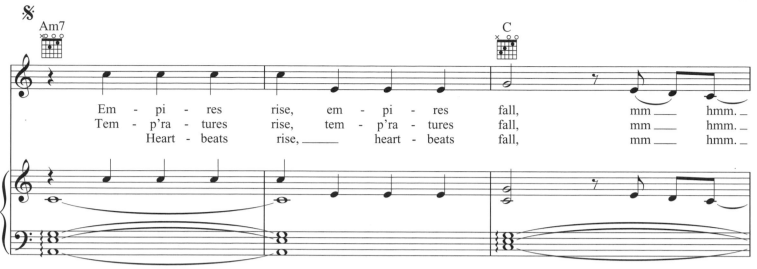

Em - pi - res rise, em - pi - res fall, mm ___ hmm. ___
Tem - p'ra - tures rise, tem - p'ra - tures fall, mm ___ hmm. ___
Heart - beats rise, ___ heart - beats fall, mm ___ hmm. ___

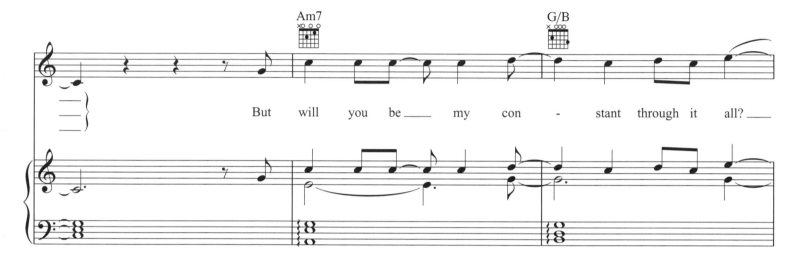

But will you be ___ my con - stant through it all? ___

I will ___ hold your ___

hand ___ and watch the world ___ spin ___ mad - ly 'round this

life we're in. _____ Oh yeah, ev - 'ry - thing goes

qui - et when it's you I'm with. _____ Oh yeah,

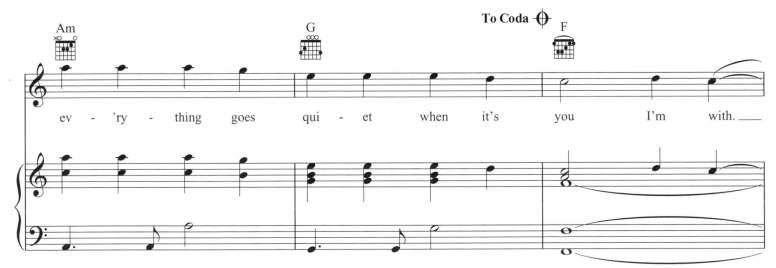

To Coda ⊕

ev - 'ry - thing goes qui - et when it's you I'm with. ____

_____ (You, you, you, you...) _____

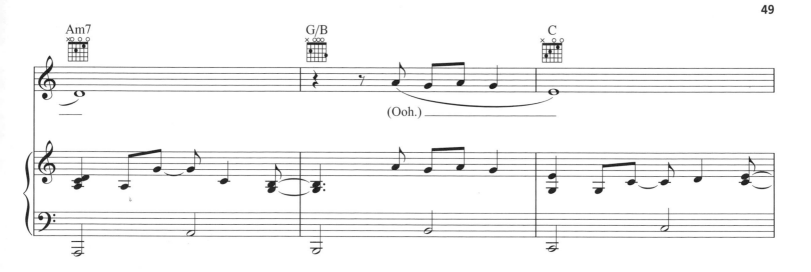

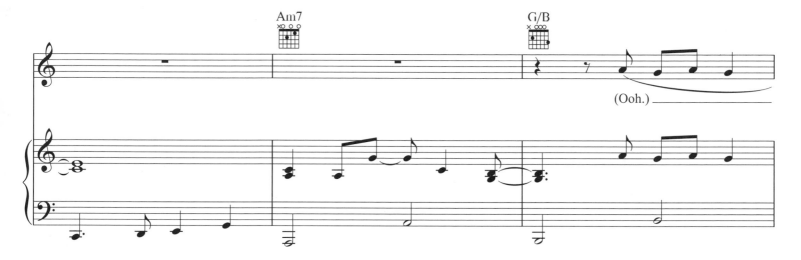

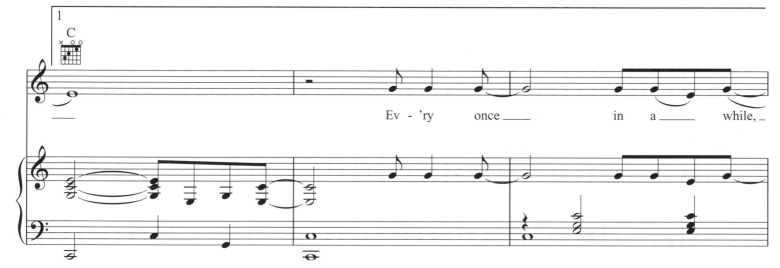

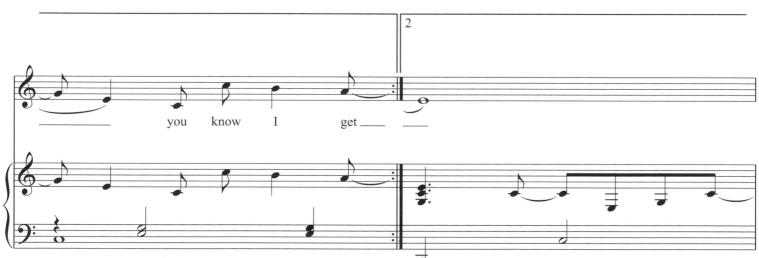

And there are no words, no

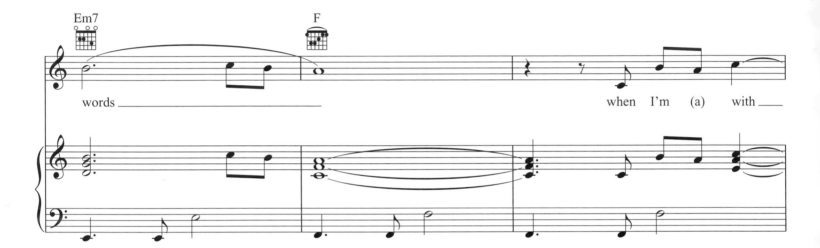

words _____ when I'm (a) with ____

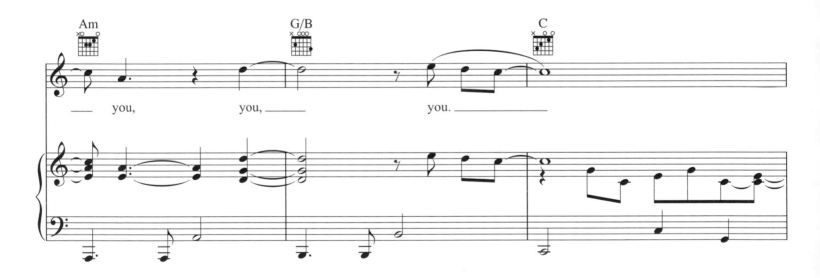

____ you, you, ____ you. ____

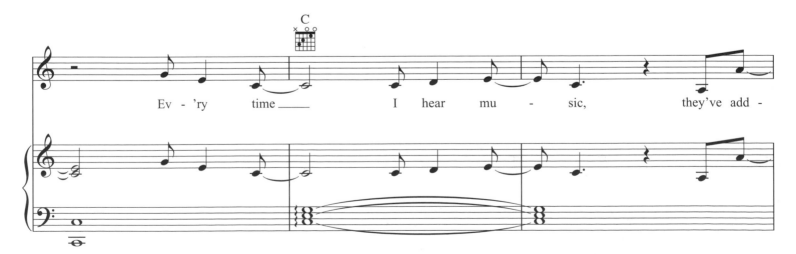

Ev - 'ry time ____ I hear mu - sic, they've add -

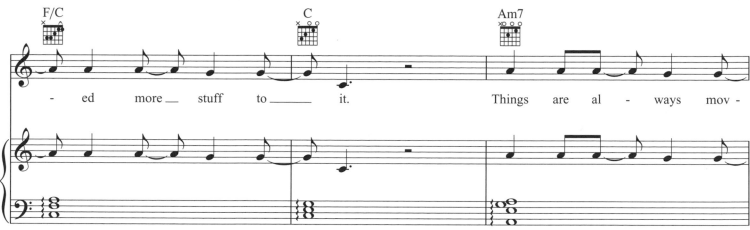

-ed more __ stuff to _____ it. Things are al - ways mov -

-ing in - to a fu - tur - is - tic place.____ Well, you and __ I, __

_____ we will try, _____ we can try to

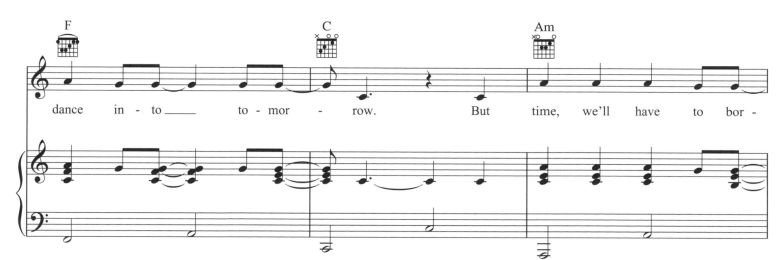

dance in - to _____ to - mor - row. But time, we'll have to bor -

D.S. al Coda

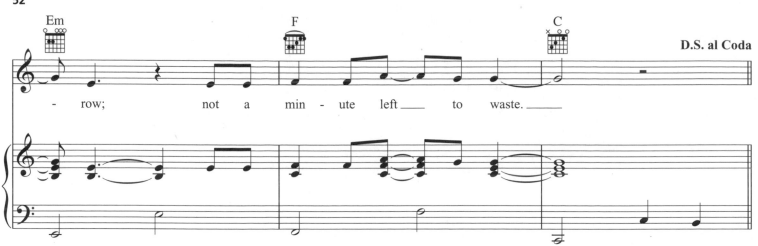

- row; not a min - ute left ___ to waste. ___

CODA

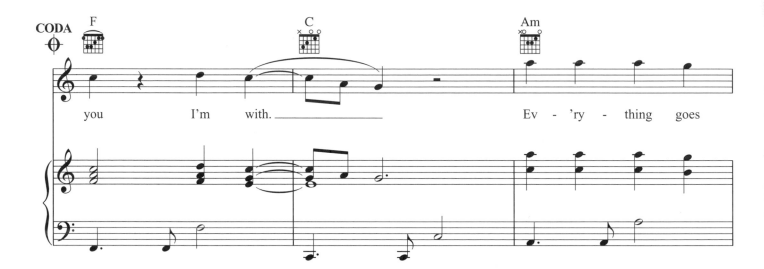

you I'm with. ___ Ev - 'ry - thing goes

qui - et when it's you I'm with. ___

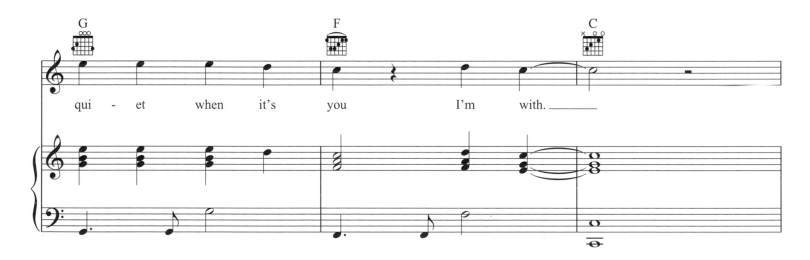

Ev - 'ry - thing goes qui - et when it's you I'm with. ___

rit.

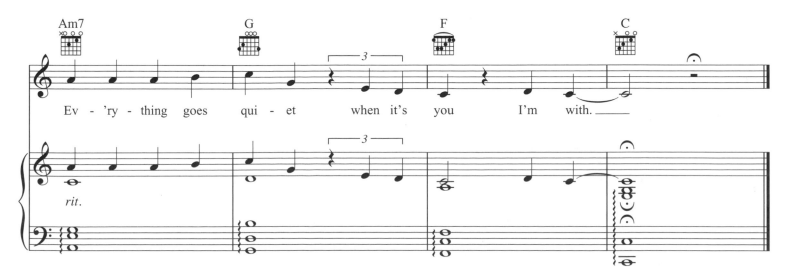

OUT OF MY HANDS

Words and Music by JASON MRAZ,
BECKY GEBHARDT, CHASKA POTTER,
MAI BLOOMFIELD and MONA TAVAKOLI

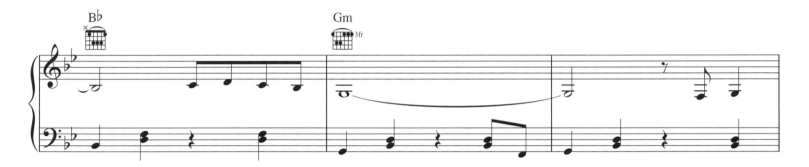

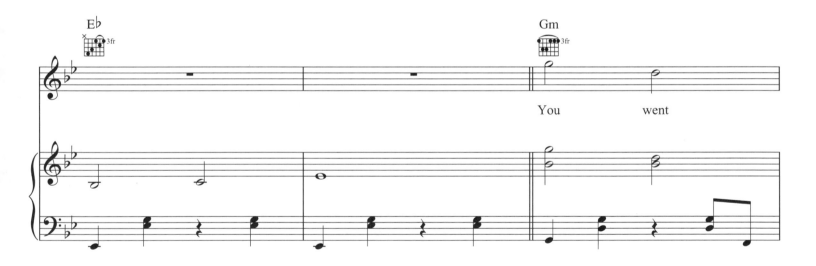

You went

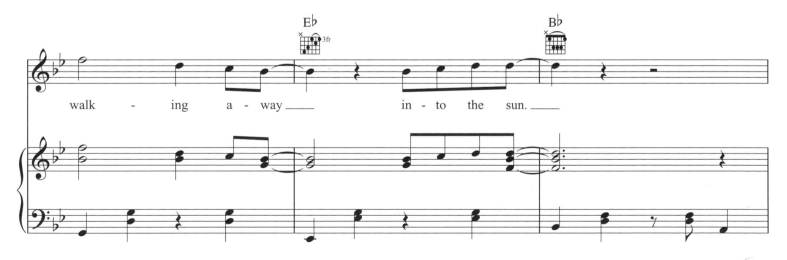

walk - ing a - way ___ in - to the sun. ___

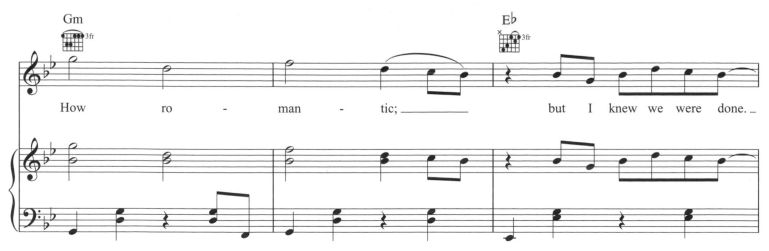

How ro - man - tic; _____ but I knew we were done. _

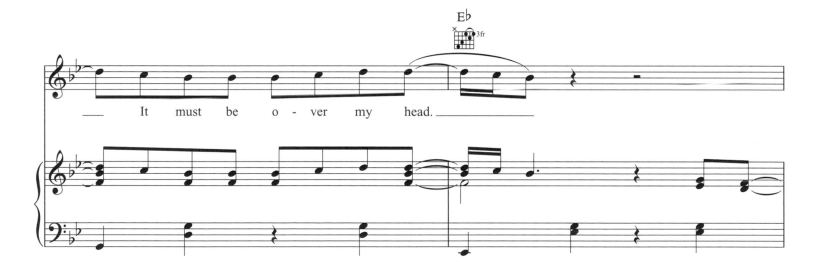

_ Was it some - thing I said? _____ Or some - thing I did? __

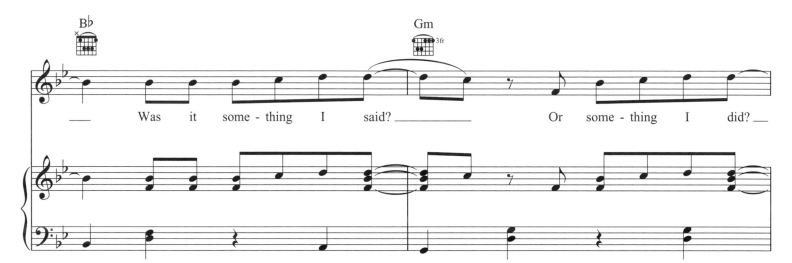

_ It must be o - ver my head. _____

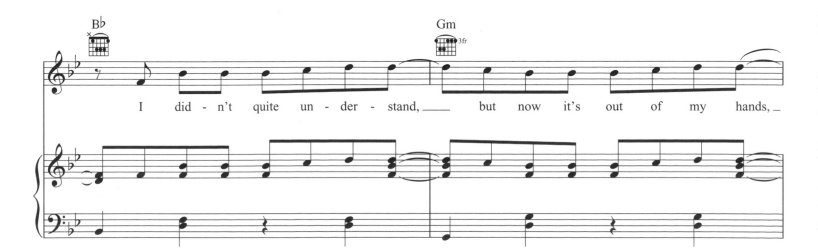

I did - n't quite un - der - stand, ____ but now it's out of my hands, _

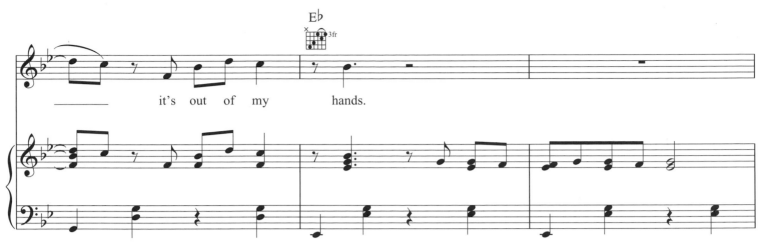

it's out of my hands.

I am sor - ry for the way you must feel a - bout your - self ev - er - y day. _

May - be you need - ed me to make it so you could keep on _

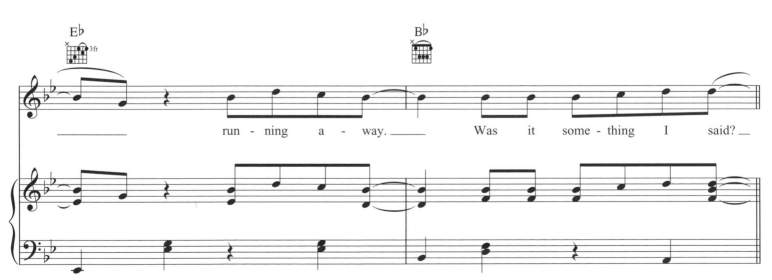

run - ning a - way. _ Was it some - thing I said? _

Gm

Or some-thing I did? _____ It must be o - ver my head. _

Eb   Bb

_____ I did - n't quite un - der - stand, _

Gm   Eb

___ but now it's out of my hands, _____ it's out of my hands.

Bb

When it feels like ___ love has got - ten out of con - trol, _

when it feels like ___ there's

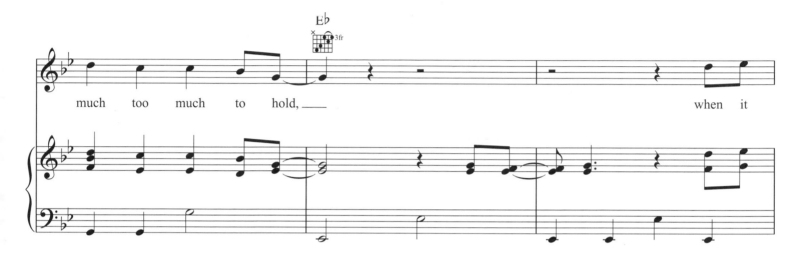

much too much to hold, ___ when it

feels like ___ too much to un - der - stand, know ___

___ that it's out of your hands, ___ out of your hands, ___ out of your hands. ___

Know ___ that it's out of your hands, ___ out of your hands, ___

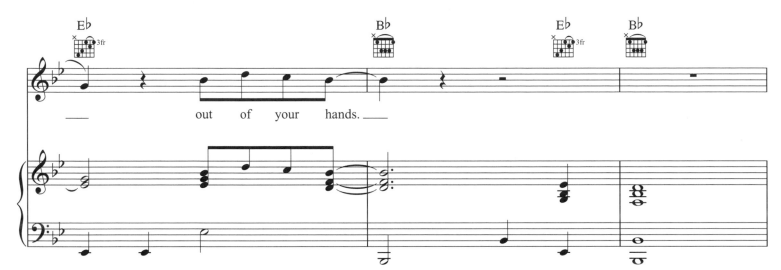

out of your hands. ___

(Ooh, _____ ooh.) _____

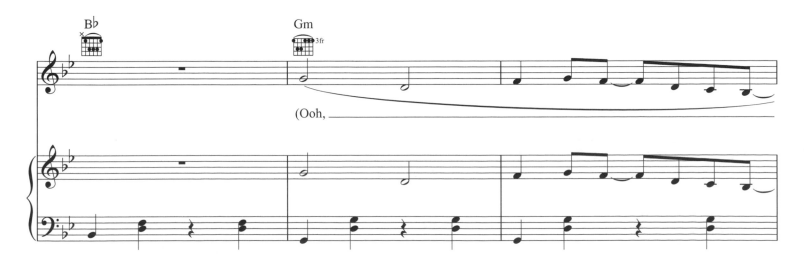

(Ooh, _____

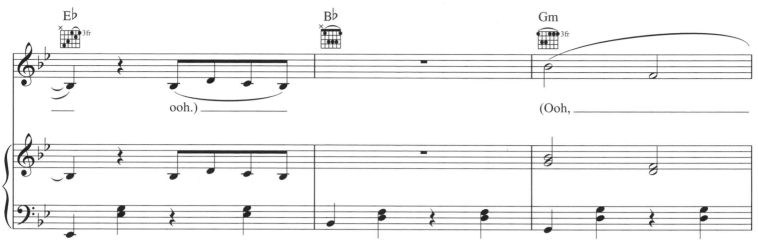

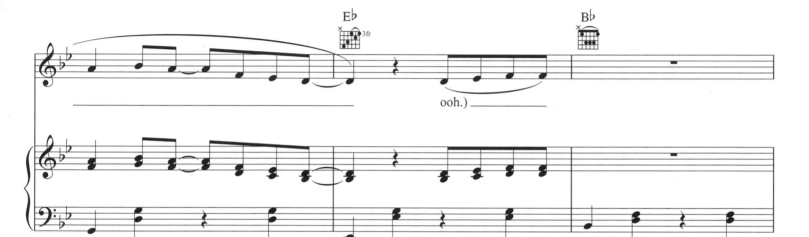

IT'S SO HARD TO SAY GOODBYE TO YESTERDAY

Words and Music by FREDDIE PERREN
and CHRISTINE YARIAN

How do I say good-bye ___ to what ___ we had? ___

The good times ___ that made us laugh ___ out-weigh the

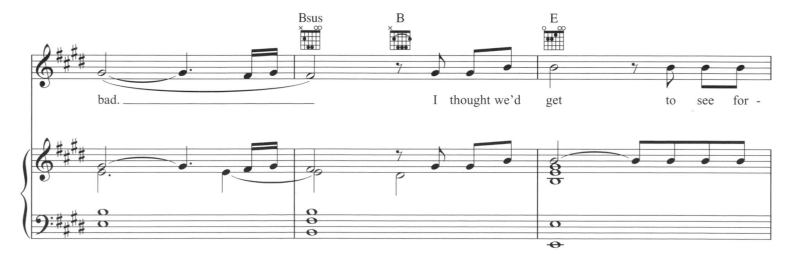

bad. ___ I thought we'd get ___ to see for-

ev - er, _____ but for - ev - er's _____ gone a - way. ___

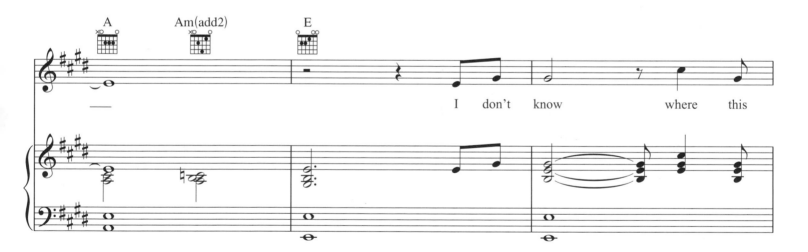

___ It's so hard to say good-bye ___ to yes - ter - day. __

___ I don't know where this

road _____ is go - ing to lead; _____ all I

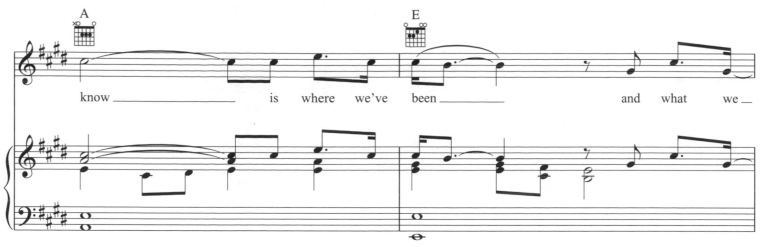

know _____ is where we've been _____ and what we _

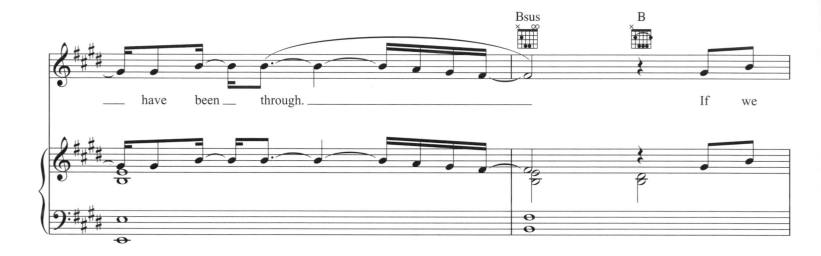

_ have been _ through. _____ If we

get _____ to see to - mor - row, _____ I hope it's worth all the

wait. _ It's so hard to say good-bye ___ to yes - ter - day. _

And I'll take with me the mem-o-ries to

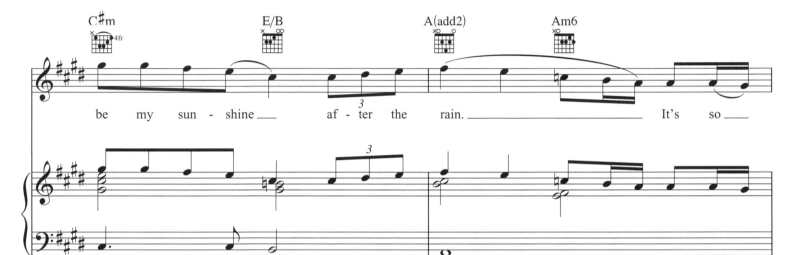

be my sun-shine ___ af-ter the rain. ___ It's so ___

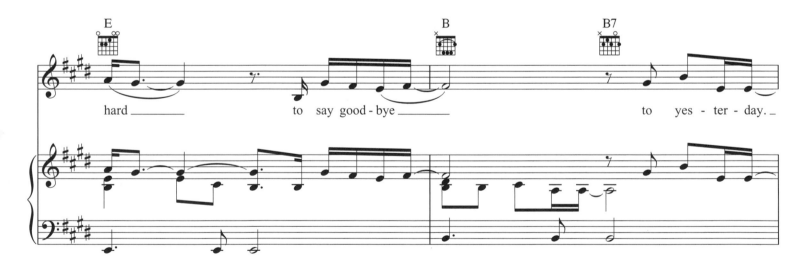

hard ___ to say good-bye ___ to yes-ter-day. ___

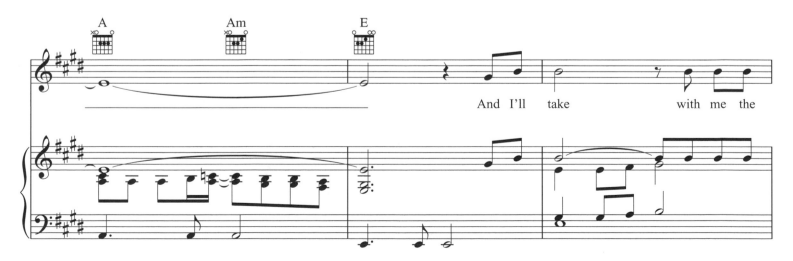

And I'll take with me the

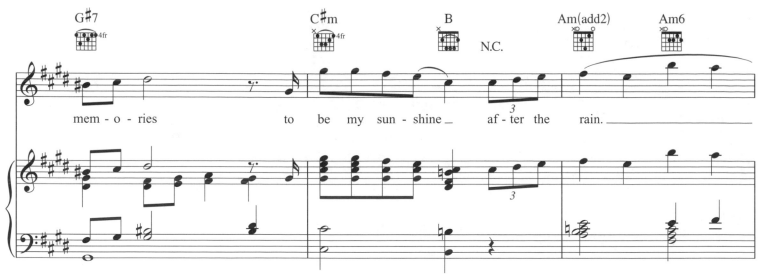

mem - o - ries   to be my sun - shine _ af - ter the rain. _

_ It's so hard   to say good-bye _   to yes - ter - day. _

_ It's so hard   to say good-bye _

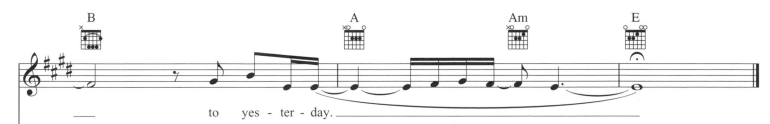

_ to yes - ter - day. _

3 THINGS

Words and Music by JASON MRAZ, MICHAEL NATTER,
NANCY NATTER, BECKY GEBHARDT, CHASKA POTTER,
MAI BLOOMFIELD and MONA TAVAKOLI

There are three things I do ___ when my life falls ___ a - part. ___

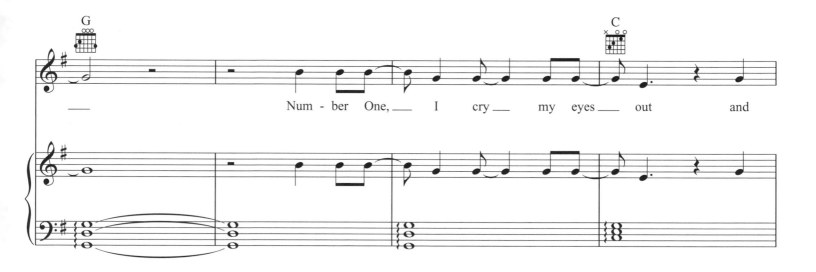

Num - ber One, ___ I cry ___ my eyes ___ out and

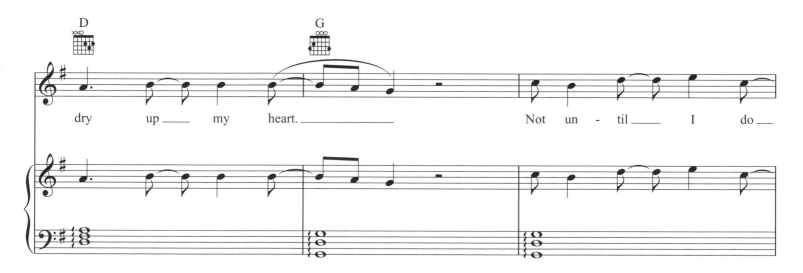

dry up ___ my heart. ___ Not un - til ___ I do ___

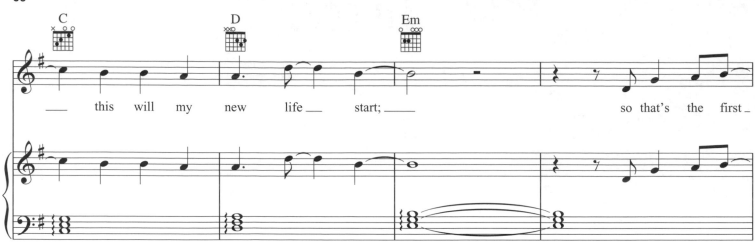

this will my new life ___ start; _____ so that's the first ___

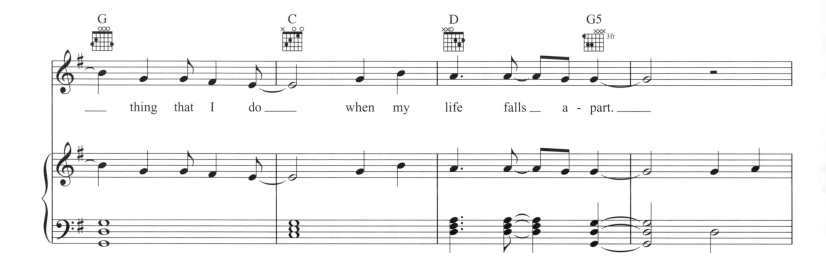

___ thing that I do _____ when my life falls ___ a - part. _____

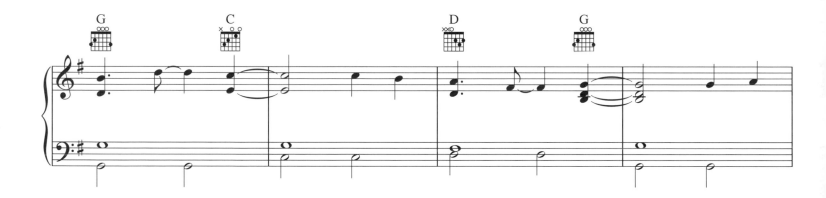

Well, the sec -

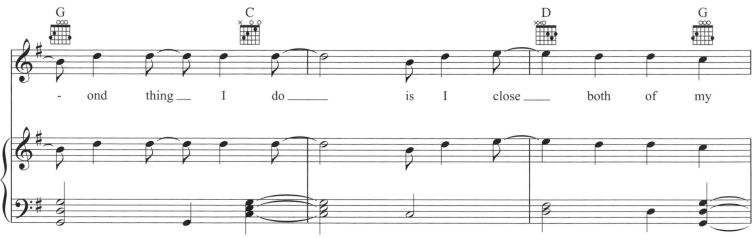

-ond thing ___ I do ___ is I close ___ both of my

eyes _____ and say my Thank ___ Yous to ___ each and ev - 'ry mo-

- ment of ___ my life. _____ I go ___ where I know that love ___

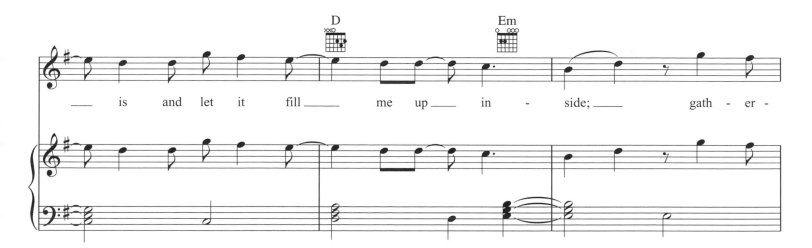

___ is and let it fill ___ me up ___ in - side; ___ gath - er-

ing the strength from sor - row, I'm glad ___ to be ___ a - live. ___

Things are look - ing up.

I know ___
I know ___

___ a - bove ___ the clouds the sun is shin - ing, ___
___ be - yond ___ the dark, the sun is ris - ing, ___

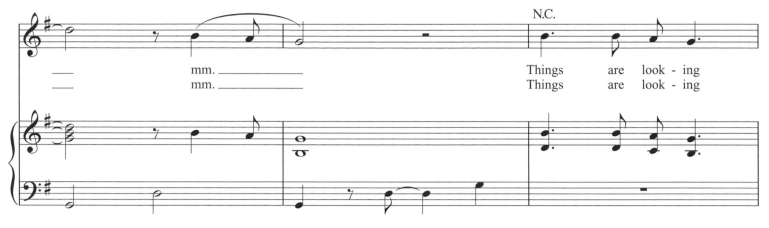

mm. _____ Things are look-ing
mm. _____ Things are look-ing

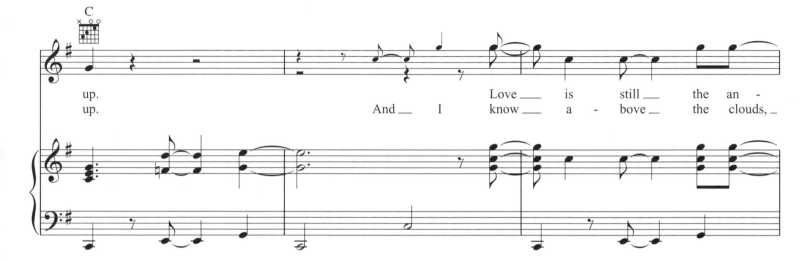

up. Love ___ is still ___ the an-
up. And ___ I know ___ a-bove ___ the clouds, ___

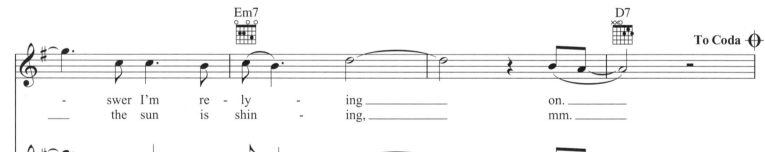

-swer I'm re-ly - ing _____ on.
___ the sun is shin - ing, _____ mm. _____

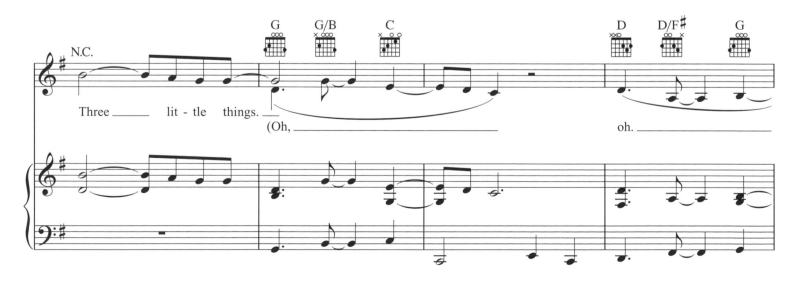

Three _____ lit-tle things. ___
(Oh, _____ oh. _____

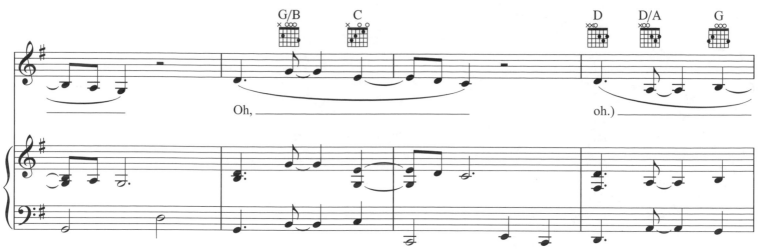

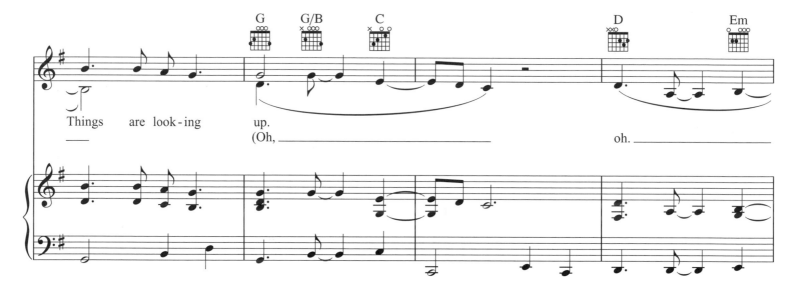

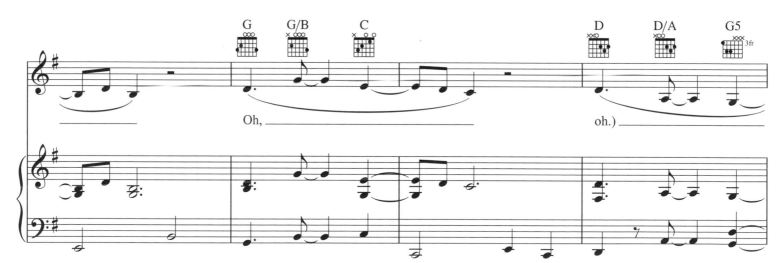

world caves __ in _____ is I pause, __ I take a breath __

__ and bow, __ and I let the chap - ter end. ____ I de -

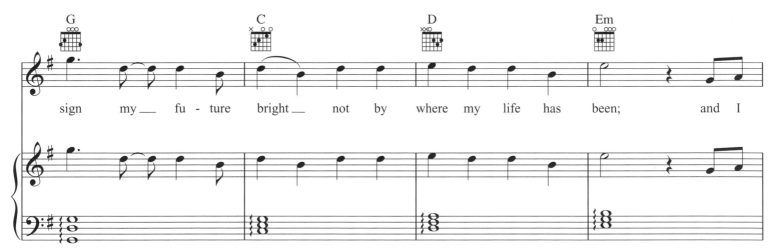

sign my __ fu - ture bright __ not by where my life has been; and I

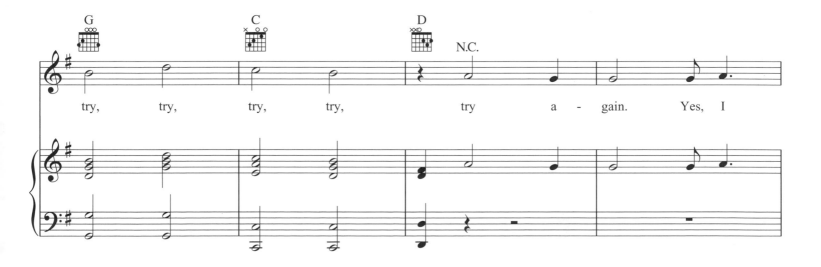

try, try, try, try, try a - gain. Yes, I

try, try, try, try,_____ try a - gain.___

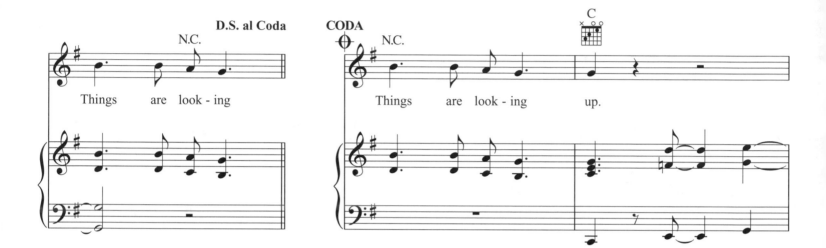

D.S. al Coda

Things are look - ing

CODA

Things are look - ing up.

Ooh,_____ love_____ is still_____ the an - swer I'm re -

ly - ing_____ on._____ Three_____ lit - tle things._

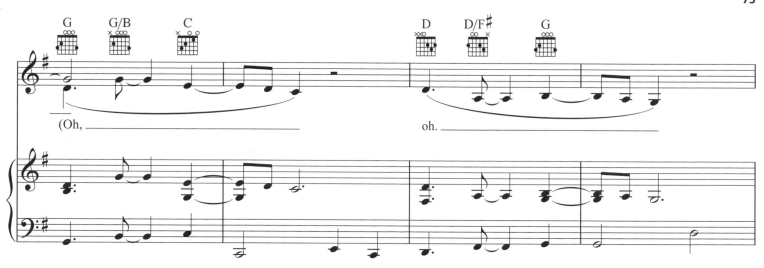

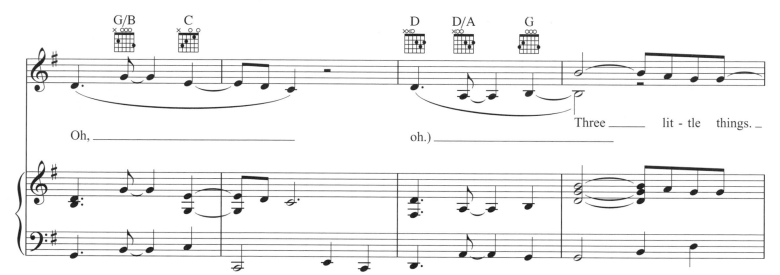

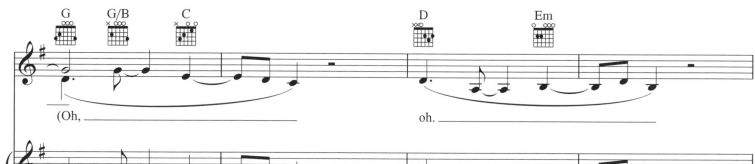

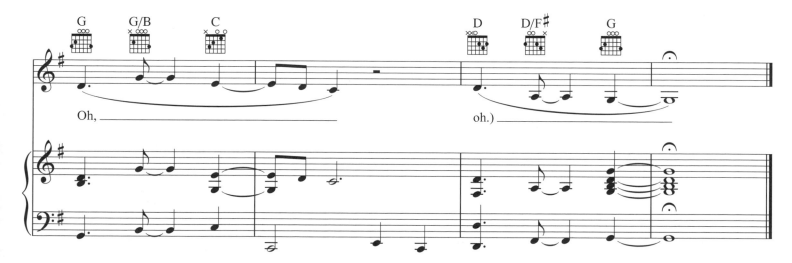

YOU CAN RELY ON ME

Words and Music by JASON MRAZ, BECKY GEBHARDT,
CHASKA POTTER, MAI BLOOMFIELD, MONA TAVAKOLI,
CHRIS KEUP, STEWART MYERS, MICHAEL NATTER
and NANCY NATTER

Some - times I rock, some - times I roll. ___
Some days are hot, some days are cold. ___

Some - times it's
Some days, we're

not me in con - trol. ___
car - ry - ing a heav - y load. ___

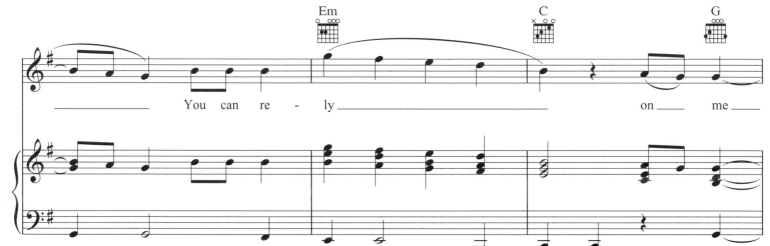

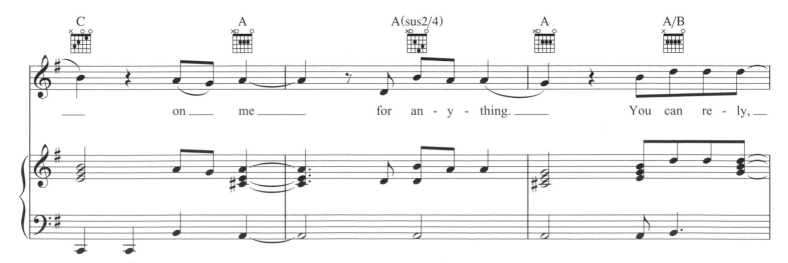

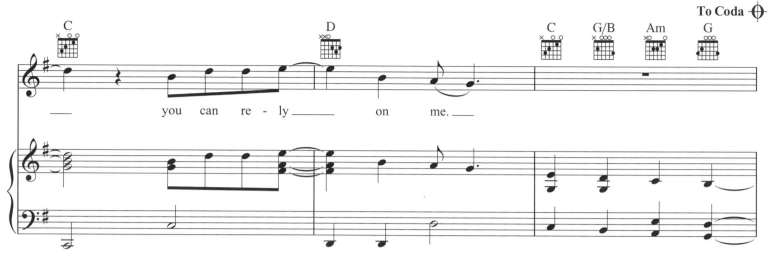

you can re - ly _____ on me. _____

And when life is hing - ing on re - gret, _____

_____ like you made up your mind _____

_____ and then you sec - ond - guessed _____ it,

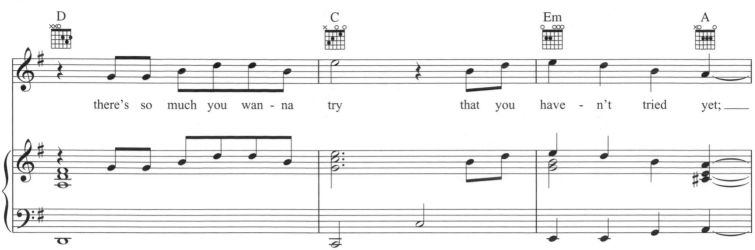

there's so much you wan-na try that you have-n't tried yet;

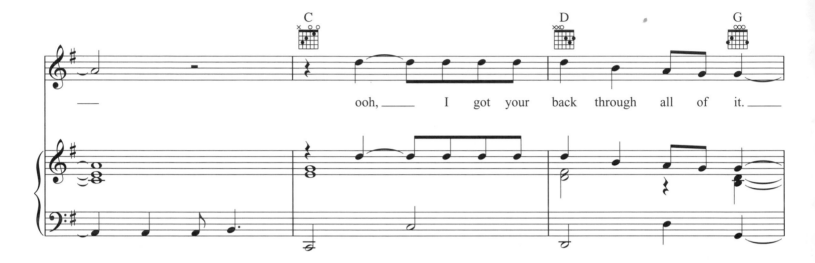

— ooh, — I got your back through all of it. —

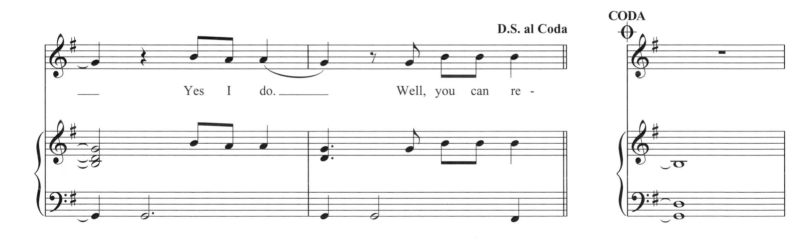

— Yes I do. — Well, you can re-

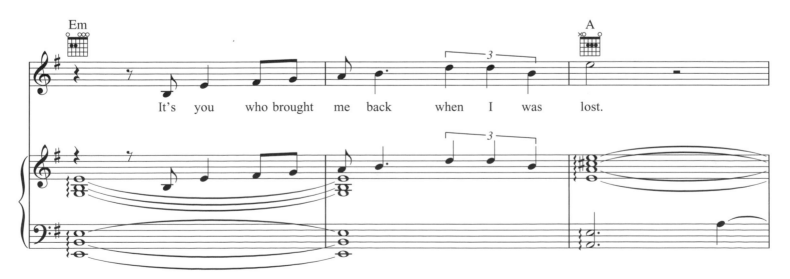

It's you who brought me back when I was lost.

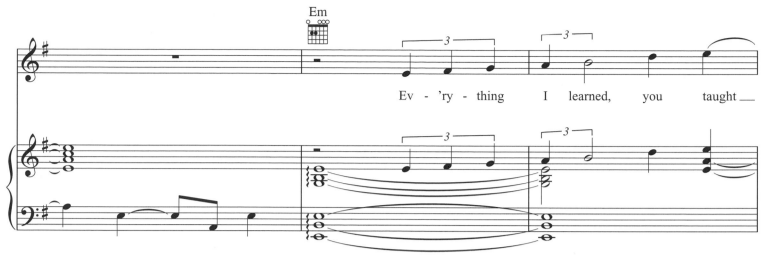

Ev - 'ry - thing I learned, you taught ___

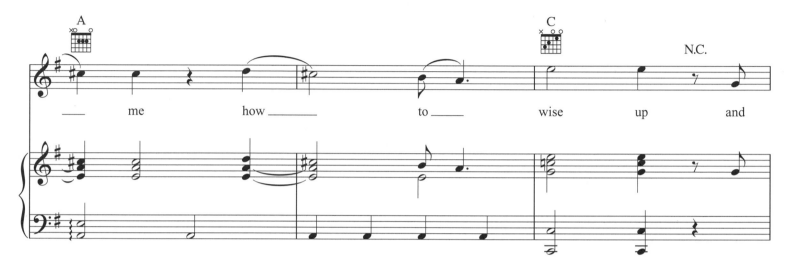

___ me how ___ to ___ wise up and

pay a lit - tle more at - ten - tion. You

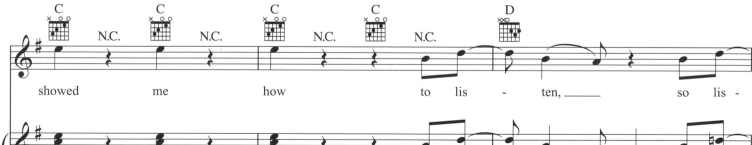

showed me how to lis - ten, ___ so lis -

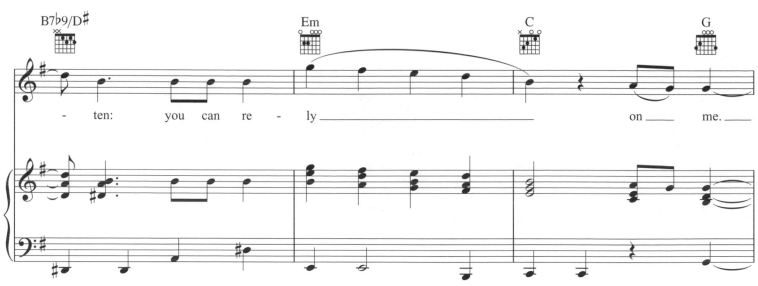

-ten: you can re- ly _____ on ___ me. ___

___ Yes you can. _____ *Instrumental solo*

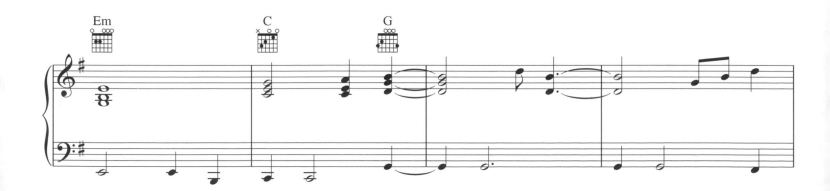

Yeah, you can re - ly _____

Solo ends

__ on ___ me. ___ Yes you can. ___ You can re -

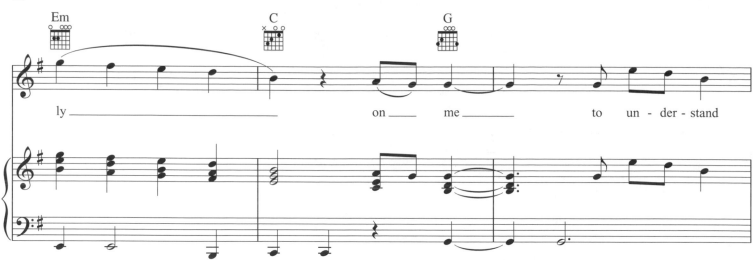

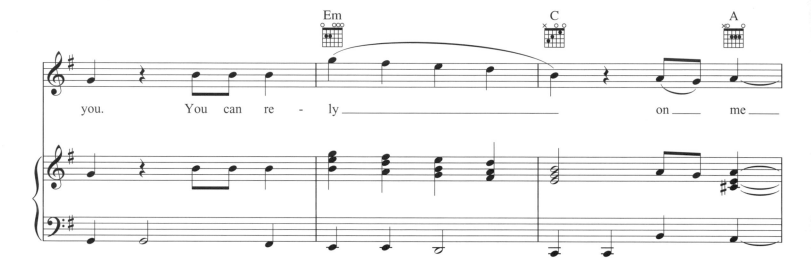

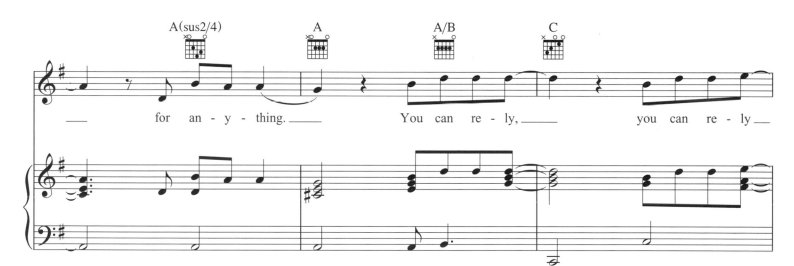

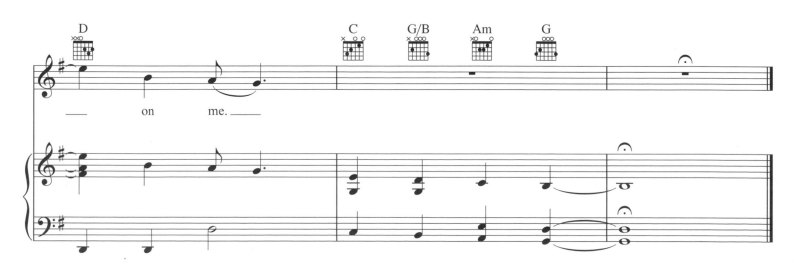

BACK TO THE EARTH

Words and Music by JASON MRAZ,
BECKY GEBHARDT, CHASKA POTTER,
MAI BLOOMFIELD and MONA TAVAKOLI

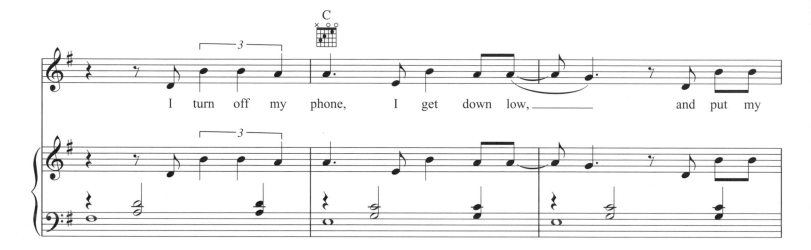

and put my feet in the grass. ___ I'm go - ing

back to the earth. ___ I'm go - ing back ___ to the earth. ___

___ I'm go - ing back _____ to work; ___ I'm go - ing back _

_____ to the earth. ___ { I'm go - ing back. _____ Doo doo doo doo doo doo

doot doot doo, __ doo doo doo doo doo doo doot doot doo, __

doo doo doo doo doo doo doot doot doo. _____

The on-ly ex-plan-a-tion for a high-rise must be that ev-

-'ry-bod-y wants to get high and move on up ___ to a de-luxe _

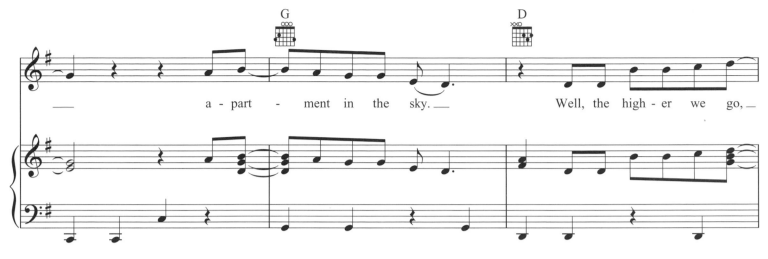

a - part - ment in the sky. ___ Well, the high - er we go, ___

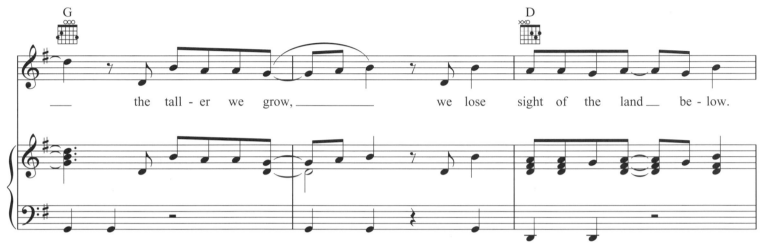

the tall - er we grow, _____ we lose sight of the land __ be - low.

Well, you can have your place ___ up in out - er space, _____ 'cause my home

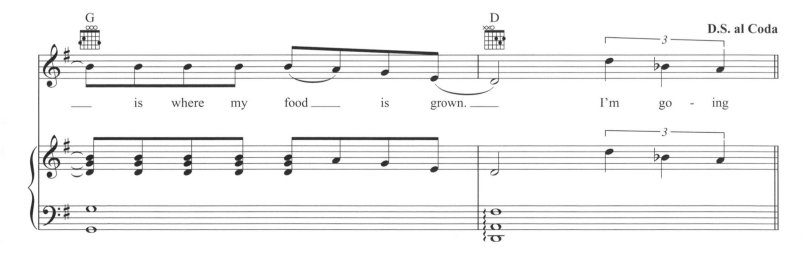

___ is where my food ___ is grown. ___ I'm go - ing

D.S. al Coda

doot doot doo. _ *Spoken: Alright, let's get jurassic on this bridge.* We are an-

-i-mals; (We are ani - i-mals;) we are wild. _ (we are wild.) _ It

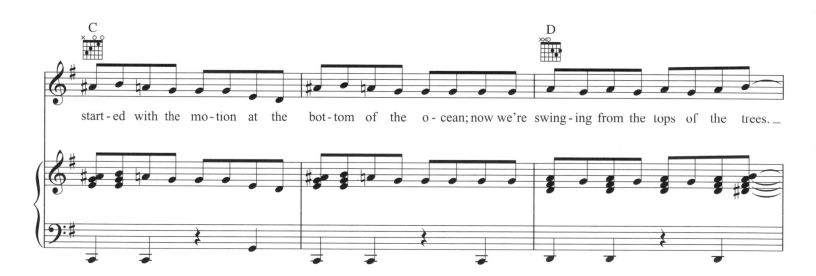

start-ed with the mo-tion at the bot-tom of the o-cean; now we're swing-ing from the tops of the trees. _

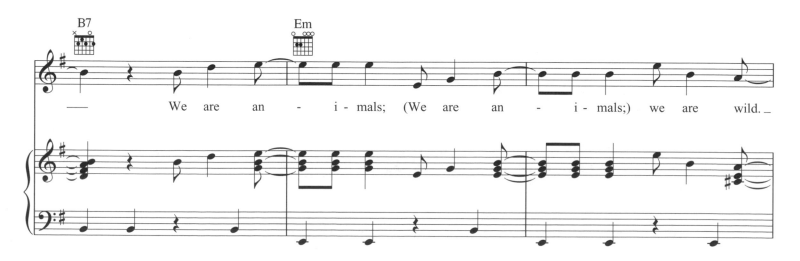

_ We are an - i-mals; (We are an - i-mals;) we are wild. _

A WORLD WITH YOU

Words and Music by JASON MRAZ,
CHRIS KEUP and STEWART MYERS

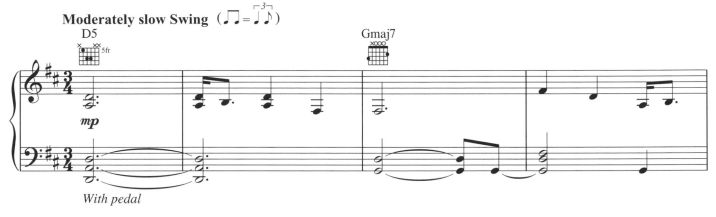

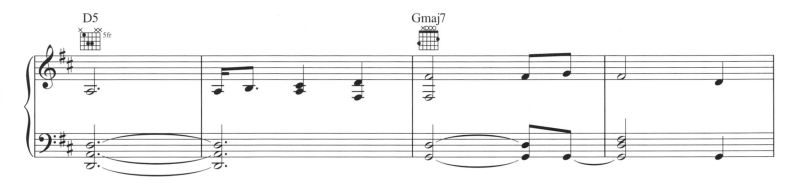

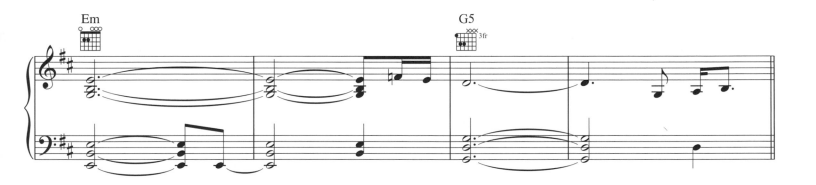

Let's   hit   the   road _____   and

throw out the map. _____ Wher - ev - er _____ we go, _____

_____ we won't look back. _____ 'Cause

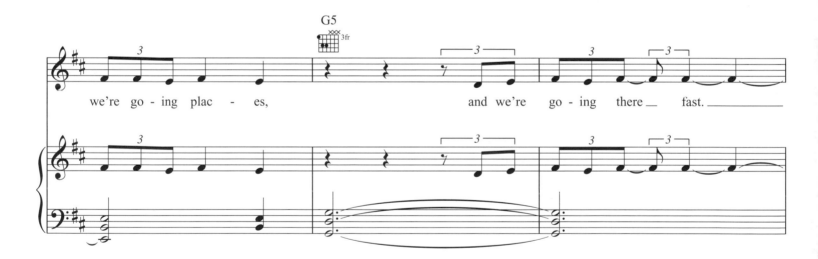

we're go - ing plac - es, and we're go - ing there _ fast. _____

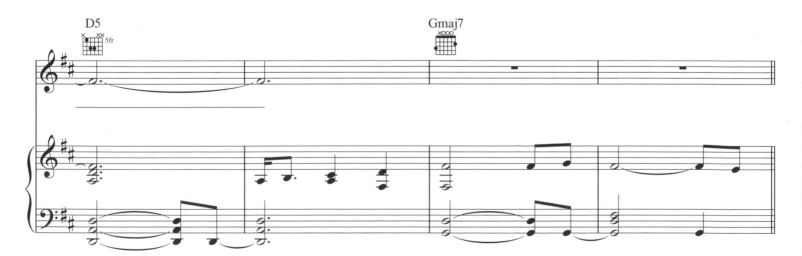

and who knows what we'll find. _____

I wan-na see the world _____ the way I _____

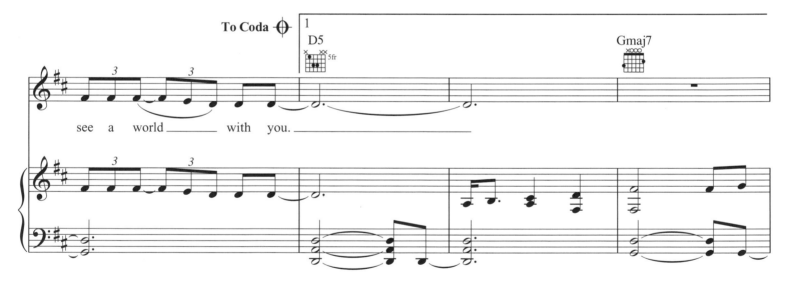

see a world _____ with you. _____

All of our prayers _____ will be an - swered. _____

The sum of all ___ our fail - ures, they can - not

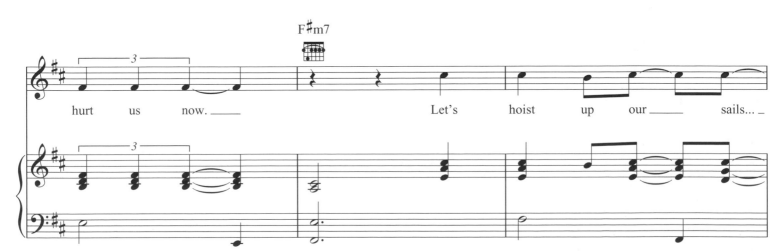

hurt us now. _____ Let's hoist up our _____ sails... _

and shove off to Chi - na and climb up a wall.

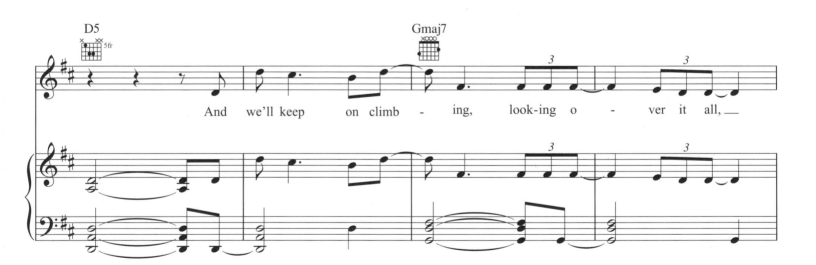

And we'll keep on climb - ing, look-ing o - ver it all, ___

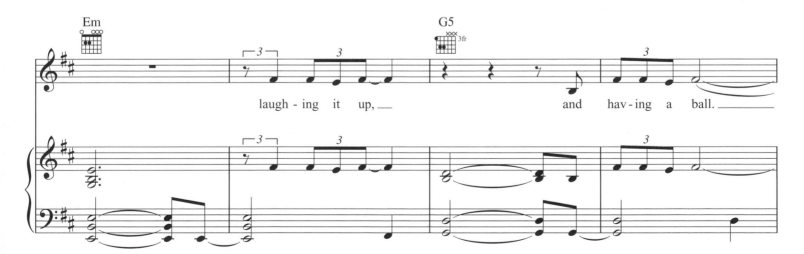

laugh - ing it up, ___ and hav - ing a ball. _____

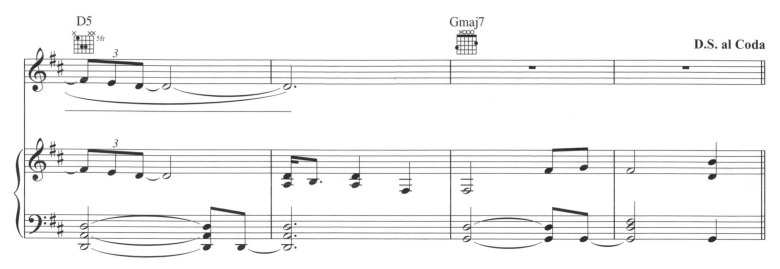

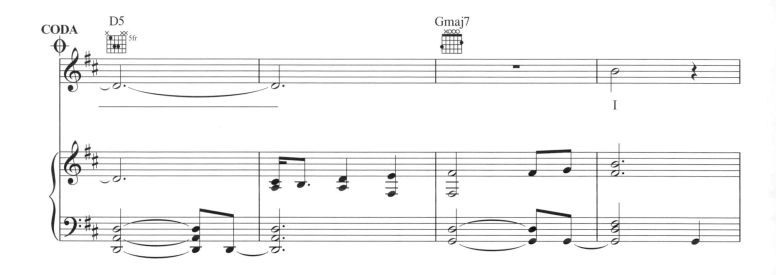

wan-na see the world _____ the way I ____ see a world ____ with you. ____

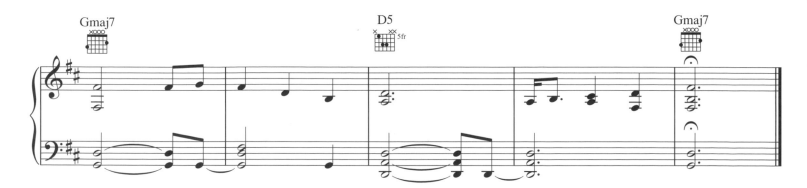

SHINE

Words and Music by JASON MRAZ, BECKY GEBHARDT,
CHASKA POTTER, MAI BLOOMFIELD
and MONA TAVAKOLI

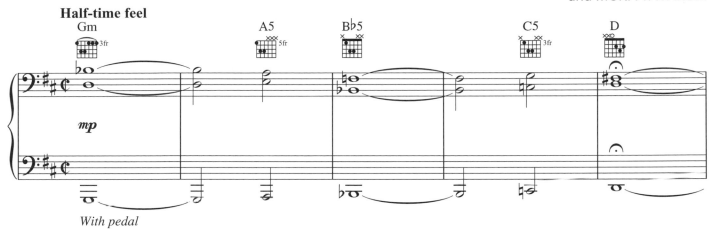

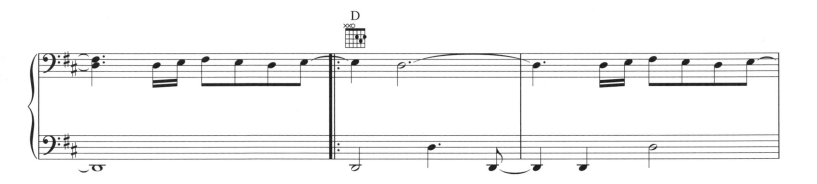

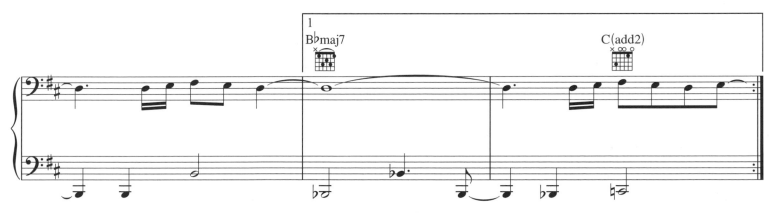

on __ you. I will shine __ on __ you." __

(Shine __ on __ you.)

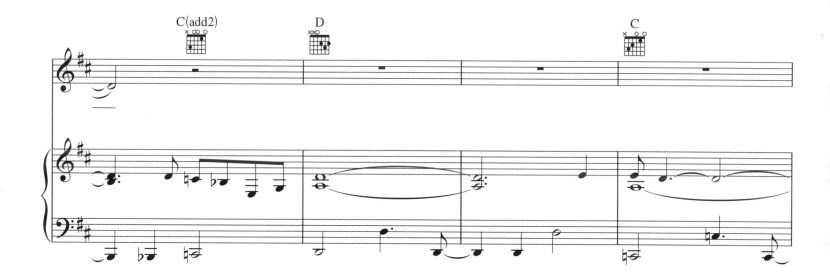

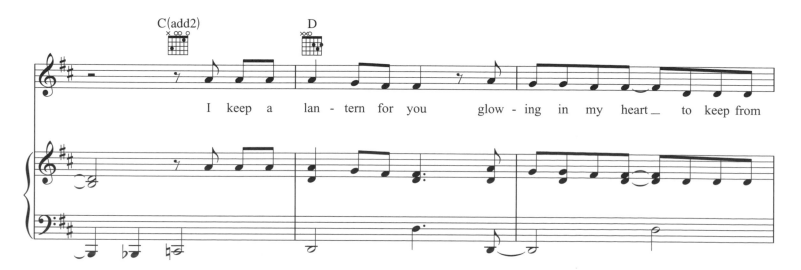

I keep a lan - tern for you glow - ing in my heart __ to keep from

you. _____

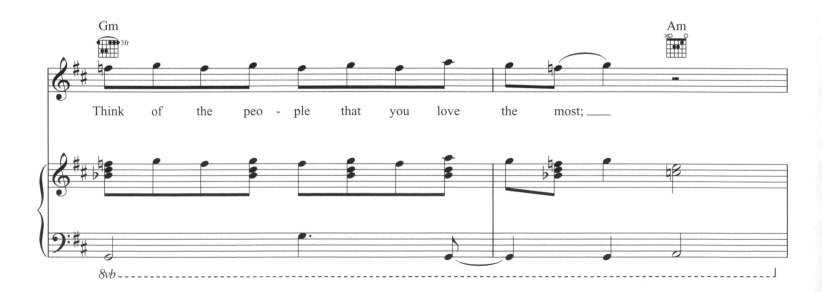

Think of the peo - ple that you love the most; ___

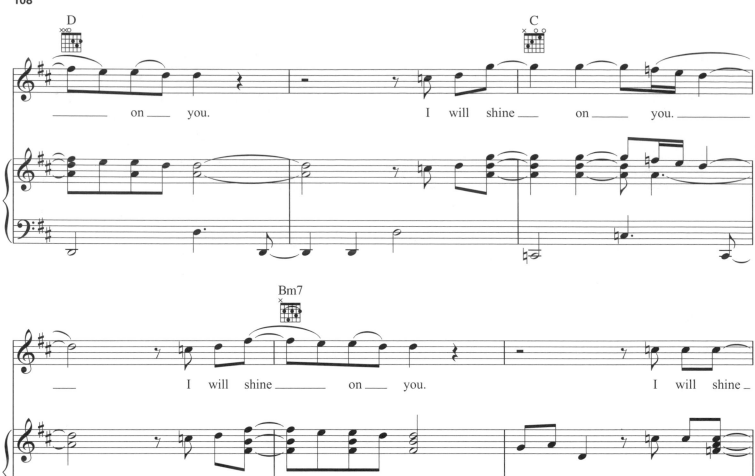

on you. I will shine on you.

I will shine on you. I will shine

on you. And if we for-get we are the

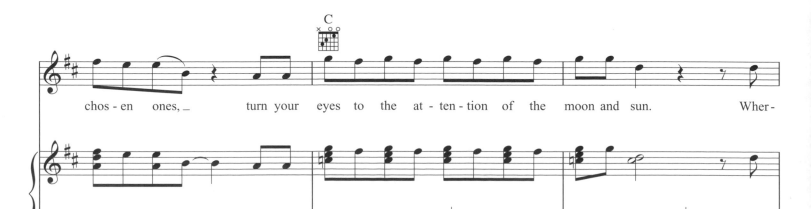

chos-en ones, turn your eyes to the at-ten-tion of the moon and sun. Wher-

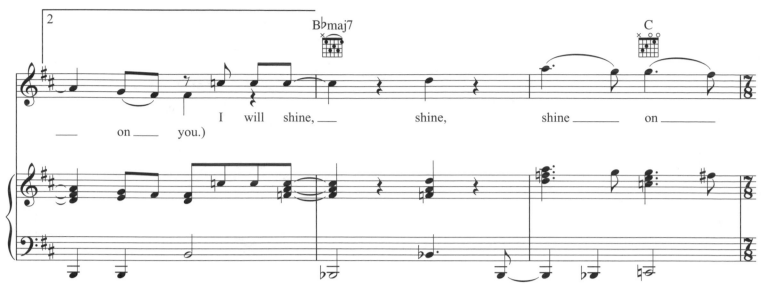

I will shine, ___ shine, shine ___ on ___
___ on ___ you.)

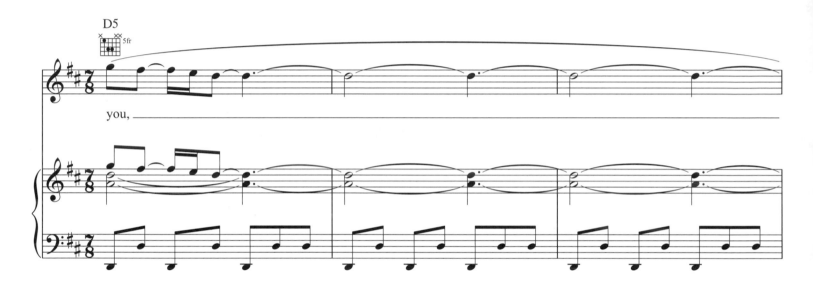

you, ___

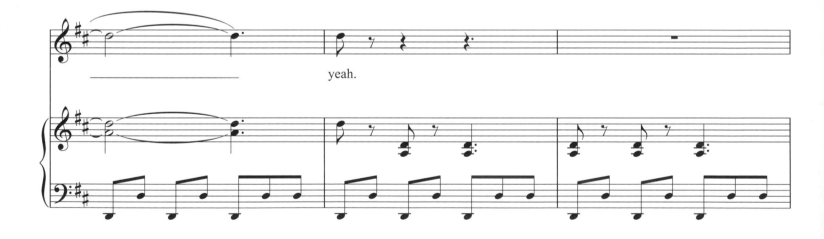

___ yeah.

(Shine __ on __ you.)

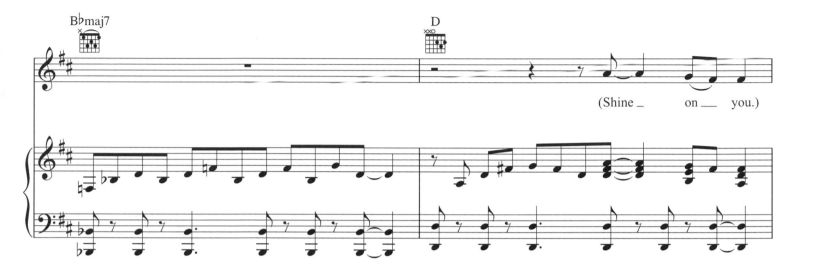

(Shine __ on __ you.)   (Shine __ on __ you.)

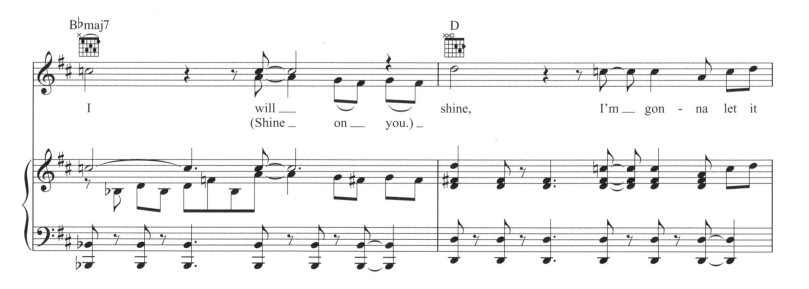

I will __ shine, I'm __ gon - na let it
(Shine __ on __ you.) __

shine, I'm __ gon - na let it shine, I'm __ gon - na let it

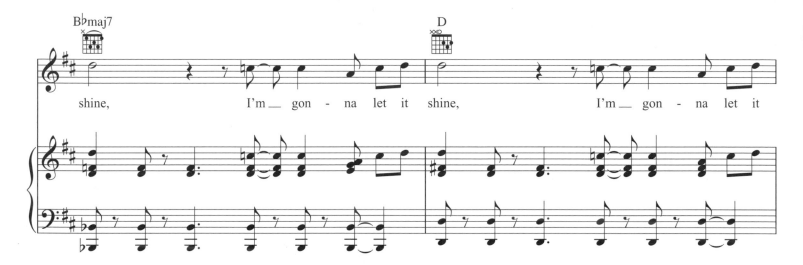

shine, I'm __ gon - na let it shine, I'm __ gon - na let it

shine, I'm __ gon - na let it shine, I'm __ gon - na let it

shine, I'm __ gon - na let it shine!